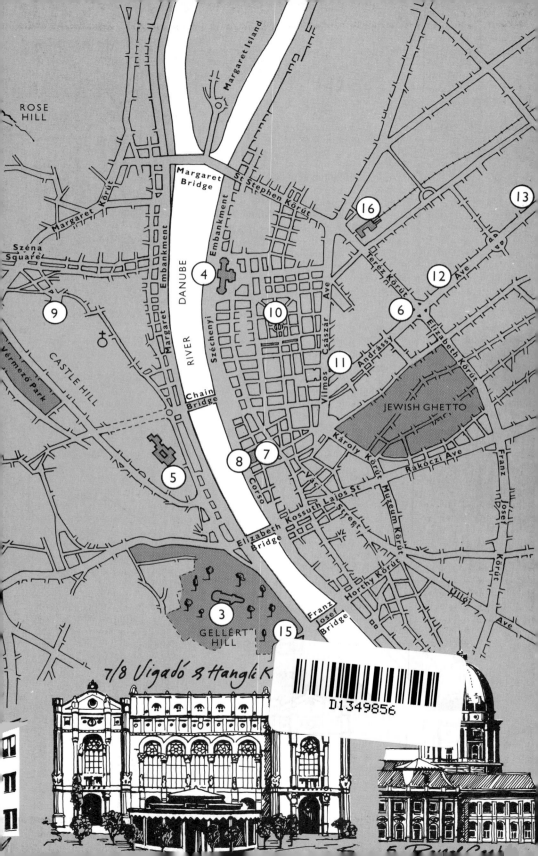

ROSE HILL

Margaret Island

Margaret Bridge

Margaret Körút

Széna Square

St Stephen Körút

Embankment

Margaret Embankment

DANUBE RIVER

Széchenyi

Chain Bridge

CASTLE HILL

Vérmező Park

Corso

Elizabeth Bridge

Vilmos

Császár Ave

Andrássy

Teréz Körút

Elizabeth Körút

JEWISH GHETTO

Károly Körút

Rákóczi Ave

Muzeum Körút

Kossuth Lajos St

Street

Horthy Körút

Franz Josef Bridge

Franz Josef Körút

Üllői Ave

GELLÉRT HILL

(4) (10) (16) (13) (12) (6) (11) (8) (7) (9) (5) (3) (15)

7/8 Vigadó & Hangli K.

D1349856

Also by Monica Porter
The Paper Bridge: A Return to Budapest

Deadly Carousel

A SINGER'S STORY OF
THE SECOND WORLD WAR

MONICA PORTER

Q

QUARTET BOOKS
LONDON   NEW YORK

For my parents

First published by Quartet Books Limited 1990
A member of the Namara Group
27/29 Goodge Street
London W1P 1FD

Copyright © Monica Porter 1990

British Library Cataloguing in Publication Data
Porter, Monica
    Deadly carousel : a singer's story of the second World War.
    1. Singing. Rácz, Vali
    I. Title
    784.092

ISBN 0 7043 2753 8

Typeset by MC Typeset Ltd, Gillingham, Kent
Printed and bound in Great Britain by
BPCC Hazell Books Ltd
Aylesbury, Bucks

With the sweetest moment of our joy
is mingled an unutterable pain

Imre Madách
The Tragedy of Man

HUNGARY
Before and After World War I

Austro-Hungarian Empire

Acknowledgements

I am grateful for the invaluable assistance given to me by the military historian and author Dr Péter Gosztonyi, of the East European Institute in Bern. He helped to clarify various historical data included in this book.

The staff of the Wiener Library in London, which specializes in the Nazi era, were most helpful to me during my research. A great deal of their material is impossible to find anywhere else, and that is why their continued existence is of such fundamental importance.

Vera Somló, Mihály Szüle and Ilona assisted me generously. And I can never repay Margit Herzog for speaking to me so openly and at length about that period of her life. I know how painful it was for her to relive her experiences and talk about the many members of her family who perished.

I thank Simon Bourgin, journalist and a family friend of very long standing, for allowing me to quote from his article, published after the war in *Life* Magazine.

Thomas Poeschel of BOA Photographic Services in Munich applied immense care and expertise to the reproduction of many of the old photographs used in this book.

My father, Péter Halász, so knowledgeable about Hungarian culture and history, told me many things I would not otherwise have known and vetted the text for inaccuracies. I'm most grateful to him.

And lastly, I want to thank my mother. For several months she was the willing and tireless victim of my questioning.

Ruthlessly I raked up her memories from nearly half a century ago, many of which she would rather have left alone. This book is a tribute to her courage.

Preface

Of the many turbulent and troubled times in the thousand-year history of the Magyar people, one year stands out in particular – from the spring of 1944 to the spring of 1945. Hungary has always been set apart from the other European countries, and its experiences during World War II were also, in certain ways, unique.

During the forties, both the Nazis and the Soviet 'liberators' were to slam down their iron fists upon the small and weakened nation. There was persecution, torture and murder, followed by its bloodthirsty sequel – more persecution, torture and murder. No one who lived through that period in Hungary can be in any doubt as to the meaning of the word 'terror'. That single year – 1944–5 – was decisive. It marked the 'changing of the guard' from Right to Left.

Looking back, it is clear that once the Golden Age of the Austro-Hungarian Empire was destroyed by the First World War and its consequence – the ruthlessly punitive measures of the Treaty of Trianon – a remarkable thing began to happen in Hungary. It was as if a vast and monstrous carousel were slowly grinding into action, a vehicle which would sweep up the country and its people and carry them ever onwards, around and around, from one calamity to another. It was relentless and inescapable as it gathered speed, and very many of those caught up in it were to perish.

This is the true and unembellished story of someone who not only survived the deadly carousel, but helped a few others survive it, too. Not a politician, diplomat or general, with powers and forces to command, but a singer: my mother.

One

Spring 1989. Budapest. The capital is a seething cauldron. There are more fundamental changes taking place in one week than previously took place in a decade. Not since the tragic uprising of 1956 has the world paid such close attention to this small, struggling nation which lies in the so-called Carpathian Basin.

The country is bankrupt and broken, the legacy of forty years of Communist totalitarianism. Lagging hopelessly behind its high-tech neighbours to the West, it has a massive debt to the Western banks which it cannot repay. Its national currency, the forint, has been losing value for years, and the poor have been rapidly growing in number.

Out of sheer desperation, the cadres are now willing to try anything to improve the situation, even something they've never tried before: democracy. But after so many years of repression, does anyone in Hungary know how it works? Since the Communist take-over in 1948, when that first post-war flowering of democracy was strangled at birth by the agents of Stalin, generations have grown up with scarcely a whiff of freedom.

But it is surprising how quickly a nation can get the hang of it. A new constitution is being written, modelled, so they say, on that of the USA. The Hungarian Parliament, encrusted with its old Party yes-men, is to be dissolved, and new, free elections held. In the countryside, the State is beginning to return to the farmers land which it took away from them decades ago. The

1

press has been unchained, and every week new, independent newspapers, magazines and publishing houses are born. The word 'defector' has fallen into disuse, as there are no defectors from a country which everyone is, apparently, free to leave.

The omnipotent Communist Party machinery is being systematically dismantled. Wherever one looks, the old guard, the dogmatists, the hated cadres, are being booted out of office. This is a people at long last wriggling out of its straitjacket.

In the midst of this unprecedented upheaval, an elderly, white-haired woman, silver-topped ebony cane in hand, is strolling slowly along the Danube promenade, together with a much younger man. It is a beautiful, balmy spring day. They pass pavement cafés and restaurants, brimming with tourists. On the Buda side of the river the Royal Castle, serene up on its hill, provides a story-book backdrop to their conversation.

The young man is a journalist, and he is carrying a tape recorder. The elderly woman was once a famous *chanteuse* and actress in Hungary. From the mid-thirties until the end of the war the name Vali Rácz was, to all Hungarians, synonymous with glamour and sophistication. They liked to compare her to another popular entertainer of the era, Marlene Dietrich.

She had emigrated to the West decades earlier, and although this is not her first return trip to Budapest, only recently have the Hungarian press and media sought her out. In fact, after years of being an official 'non-person', she is now in the middle of a full-scale revival. Radio and television interviews, articles in the papers, the release of an LP of many of her old recordings, and, as a culmination, the planned opening of a Vali Rácz 'museum' in the near future. Fan mail is beginning to arrive at the Gellért Hotel, where she is known to stay during her visits. Requests for autographed photos. Just like in the old days.

Nostalgia is not only extremely fashionable, but plays a vital part in this present climate of 'anything goes' – the very idea of admitting to nostalgia for pre-Communist days would have been unthinkable a year or two ago. Listening to old wartime records, even privately, was strictly forbidden. Now they are being broadcast on national radio. The old films, condemned as

2

capitalist and bourgeois, which had been locked away in the archives, are being dusted off and shown on TV and in the cinema with enormous success.

'Speak about anything,' the young man says, 'anything that comes to mind. Memories, fragments, images from the past.'

'But why are you so interested in all these details?'

'We're interested in everything, we want to know about everything, because for four decades they've been lying to us. They rewrote our history, stole our past. Now, at last, we have the chance to retrieve it − to put together all those missing pieces, and see things as they really were.'

Imperceptibly, he switches on his tape recorder.

Two

Spring 1944. Budapest. A quiet Sunday morning. A taxi pulled up before the grand old Vigadó concert hall near the riverfront where posters advertised a concert for 10.45 that morning, 19 March: Chappy, the 'King of Jazz', and his 'world famous' Moulin Rouge Orchestra were due to play, with guest appearances by several popular singers.

One of them, Vali Rácz, now stepped out of the taxi. But she told the driver to wait. There was something wrong. A notice had been fixed on to the entrance of the Vigadó – *This concert has been cancelled.* All the doors were locked and, when Vali hammered on them, there was no response from within. Perplexed and anxious, she returned to the taxi and told the driver to take her back home.

From her villa on Budakeszi Avenue she made a few hurried phone calls, and soon learned the reason for the concert's cancellation. That day the Nazi war machine had finally, and catastrophically, engulfed the Hungarian nation.

It was code-named 'Operation Margarethe': at 2 a.m. on 19 March 1944, eleven divisions of the Wehrmacht moved into Hungary from all four directions and, encountering virtually no resistance, within twelve hours had occupied every town and village. Matters were now in the hands of the all-powerful Edmund Veesenmayer, newly-appointed Reich Plenipotentiary for Hungary. Equally sinister was the arrival at the same time of the Gestapo, who proceeded at once to arrest hundreds of prominent Jews and political figures suspected of sympathizing

4

with the Allied cause and of being involved in the Hungarian government's attempt to switch sides during the war. That, after all, was one of the two reasons for the German occupation.

The other reason was to solve at last the 'Jewish problem' in Hungary. For years, while all around them the Jewish communities of Europe had been gradually annihilated in the death camps, the 800,000 Jews of Hungary had been living in a haven. And many thousands of Jews from neighbouring countries had also escaped death by seeking refuge in Hungary. Successive Hungarian governments, under the relatively benign (if blinkered) rule of Regent Nicholas Horthy, had failed to carry out the deportations for so long urged by Berlin. Now the Nazis would wait no longer.

SS-Obersturmbannführer Adolf Eichmann, of the Reich Security Main Office, arrived in Budapest two days after the Wehrmacht, with his 'Special Operations Commando'. He had one mission to accomplish: the complete liquidation of Hungarian Jewry. He had already implemented the final solution in his previous postings throughout Europe, and now he was bristling and confident as he turned his hand to Hungary.

Personally, Vali Rácz had nothing to fear. Her origins were, in the Nazi nomenclature, 'impeccably Aryan'. But, as even she did not yet suspect, her life was to be intricately bound together with the fate of the now-hunted Jews.

Operation Margarethe also doomed Budapest itself, earmarked it for destruction, by turning it into one of the fiercest arenas of war. Never again would it be the same. Before the war it was a glittering international capital, with the most fabulous nightlife and the finest hotels and cafés to be found anywhere in Europe. It was an elegant, stylish city, renowned for its chic women. It wasn't by mere chance that in the 1930s Budapest had been the favourite adventure playground of, among others, the Prince of Wales, whose escapades in the city were famous. One of his haunts was the sensational Arizona nightclub, owned by a woman known simply as 'Miss Arizona'. Here he would order one *barack pálinka* after the other (the famous Hungarian peach brandy: his favourite drink) while watching Miss Arizona perform with her snakes, or ride around the stage on the back of a baby elephant.

From 1935, when Vali Rácz graduated from the Music Academy of Budapest, she, too, was an integral part of this sophisticated nightlife. Straight away her career took off. Radio and recording contracts, concerts, roles in plays and films, regular singing engagements in cafés and nightclubs – the offers fell into her lap. It wasn't difficult to see why. She had a superb, trained singing voice, an incandescent beauty, and she worked very hard.

She had a house built beside the green hills of Buda, on the other side of the Danube from the noise and crowds of Pest, and furnished it richly with antiques. Around it she created a lush garden. She had a live-in housekeeper, a maid, and a secretary to deal with correspondence, including the fan mail. In short, she was a star, and she lived like one.

She made eighteen films between 1936 and 1943, and perhaps it was inevitable that she was typecast in all of them as the *femme fatale*, the seductress, the 'other woman'. She was so convincing in that role. She looked too sexy ever to be the heroine, and besides, she had a habit in her films of deceiving nice men, slapping the maid, losing her temper and smashing things against the wall. A dangerous woman to know.

Who would have guessed that this Budapest *mondaine*, oozing *haute couture* gloss and glamour, was not the product of the great capital at all, but of a tiny peasant village in southwest Hungary, in the district known as the Dunántúl – Transdanubia?

Valéria Rácz was born in Gölle, in Somogy County, on Christmas Day 1911, during the closing chapter of the Austro-Hungarian Empire. A period which had begun with the 'Compromise' with Austria in 1867 had turned out to be a Golden Age for Hungary, a time of liberal reforms, progress and prosperity. With its pre-1918 borders, Hungary was a vast polyglot kingdom, tolerant of its various minorities: Swabian Germans, Slovaks, Croatians, Serbs, Rumanians, Jews. And although Budapest and Vienna were the Empire's twin capitals, Hungarian culture was in some ways influenced more by England and France than by Austria.

Vali's father, Ferenc Rácz, was headmaster at the village

6

school in Gölle and cantor at its old Catholic church. A well-known and respected local figure, he was well versed in art and literature, and was considered to have the finest tenor singing voice in the Dunántúl. He was once offered a scholarship to study operatic singing in Italy, but decided against it, choosing to stay in Gölle with his wife and small daughter. He realized soon enough that his daughter had inherited his musical talent, and encouraged her to be the one to make a career out of it.

On the day Vali was born, he returned home from church, where he'd played the organ and led the singing during Christmas Day mass, to find he had a daughter instead of the hoped-for son. But he quickly reconciled himself to it, and sitting down at the piano with the newborn baby on his lap, he placed her little fingers on the keys. A prophetic gesture, as it turned out.

Ferenc Rácz, too, had an origin which would have surprised many who knew this cultured, educated man. His own father, far from being either artistic or in a learned profession, had been a wealthy peasant farmer – known pejoratively as a *kulak* in later Soviet terminology – the owner of 300 hectares in the neighbouring county of Tolna. Ferenc, born in 1884, was the youngest of twelve children, and the only one to have no desire at all to live a peasant's life.

At fourteen he ran away from his father's estate, and was befriended by the parish priest in a village some distance away. More than anything else, he had a yearning for education, and the priest became a kind of mentor to him. Eventually, Ferenc's parents relented and allowed him to lodge with the priest, paying for his maintenance. The priest undertook to supervise his education, which he did conscientiously. In time, Ferenc was enrolled in the teacher-training college in Győr, where he also learned to paint, and began to acquire his library of Hungarian literature.

In 1910, he met and married eighteen-year-old Gizella Sohonyay. Her father's family belonged to the old Hungarian gentry. Her maternal ancestors, the Nettlaus, were a family of well-to-do bakers. They had come from Prussia in the

7

eighteenth century when Queen Maria Theresa encouraged German settlement of Hungary where the population had been decimated by 150 years of tyrannical Turkish rule.

Ferenc and Gizella moved to Gölle, where he took up the post of cantor/teacher. Not every Hungarian village had a school, but in Gölle there had been once since time immemorial. He was very religious, and this may have been at least partly due to the fact that it was the Church, in the form of his erstwhile priest-mentor, which had provided him with an escape route from the peasant life, and the alternative he so desperately sought.

His eleven brothers and sisters, none of whom received higher education, never forgave him for what they viewed as his preferential treatment, nor for the way in which he had 'deserted' his family. Later, when the paterfamilias died and his land and assets were divided between them, Ferenc was disinherited. He had nothing to do with his siblings after that.

Those early years in Gölle, in the sunset of the Empire, were to leave powerful and lasting impressions upon Vali. It was a wondrous life for a child in the headmaster's thick-walled, L-shaped house, built by Franciscan monks three hundred years before. It was heated in winter with wood-burning tiled stoves, and for light, in those days before electricity, they had hanging 'Aladdin lamps' which burned petroleum and gave the rooms, with their Gothic arches, a warm, reddish glow. In summer it was surrounded by an exotic paradise of a garden, tended by the headmaster himself.

Part of the headmaster's salary was paid in kind: Ferenc Rácz was given the use of twenty hectares for his own purposes. With a natural mastery he turned it into a flourishing model farm, where he bred livestock and produced an abundance of wheat, barley, rye and oats, corn and potatoes. There was a comprehensive kitchen garden, an orchard and a vineyard. Their surplus produce was sold in the nearby market towns.

The aromas of that childhood were particularly unforgettable – the rows of hams and sausages smoking in the smokehouse; bread and cakes baking in the kitchen; the incomparable apples which grew in the orchard; and on Christmas Eve, when the village church was decorated with Christmas trees aglow with countless candles, the intoxicating scent of pine.

In this Arcadian world, each season revealed its own wonders to the headmaster's pretty, blonde daughter – like waking up early one spring morning to find a basketful of newborn chicks lying beside her on the bed; and riding through snow-covered fields in a horse-drawn sleigh, bells ringing and with heated bricks to warm her feet, to visit relatives in the nearby town of Kaposvár. The summer meant picnics, with endless drinks of pure, cool water from the local spring. And in the autumn there would be hours of climbing apple, plum and cherry trees, to sample the season's new fruit, and long rides on top of the loaded haycart.

Although Vali was an only child, she was not a lonely one. Besides her parents, there was her beloved Aunt Karolin, her mother's younger sister, who lived with them for several years (until 1917, when she married an up-and-coming young politician and moved near to Budapest) and was like another mother to her. The two sisters got on very well, although they were so different. While Gizella had dark hair and grey eyes, and was rather stern in temperament, Karolin was blonde and blue-eyed, with a soft nature which made her much loved by everyone.

Vali made close friendships in the village, some of which were to last a lifetime. And then there was a constant array of pets and farm animals to keep her company. The favourite dog of Vali's childhood was a St Bernard, a rare sight in Hungary, which was named Lloyd after Lloyd George, the British prime minister of the day. But she even knew each pig by name, until it was slaughtered.

The land of the Dunántúl was rich and fertile. It was not by accident that the Piarist teaching order of priests had established their vast and hugely successful agricultural estate in the area around Gölle, and had their administrative headquarters in the largest and grandest building in the village. The Piarists, with their highly skilled and advanced techniques of farming and livestock breeding, exerted an important influence on the village, and, lifting it out of obscurity, turned it into a major agricultural centre of Hungary. The astute peasants of Gölle regularly produced prize-winning breeding animals in national competitions, and the fields were overflowing with produce. Until, of course, the Communists took over and the Piarists were kicked off their estate, the farms were nationalized, and the whole thing went into a rapid decline. But that was much later, in a different era altogether. Before the First World War shattered the established order in the Hungarian kingdom, it seemed as if the idyll would last forever.

When she was four years old Vali began to take piano lessons, agreeing to them only if she could ride to the piano on the back of her teacher, who had to get on his hands and knees and pretend to be a horse. At ten she was sent to a convent school in the nearby town of Dombovár. It was the end of the easy village life and the beginning of a decade of being brought up and taught by nuns, a decade in which she honed those vital traits – an iron discipline, dedication of purpose and self-restraint – which not only helped to secure her later success as a singer and actress, but helped to save her life.

She carried on with her musical studies throughout her convent years: in Dombovár, Kaposvár and for two years in the ancient town of Zwettl, in the Austrian Alps, where she was sent because of a minor lung ailment. She was skilful at the piano, but it was her singing voice – a rich, resonant mezzo-soprano – which at once captivated all who heard it. She had already performed at many school concerts and local social gatherings when one day, a few months after her graduation from the Kaposvár Girls' Gymnasium, she was asked to sit down at the piano and entertain a guest at the Rácz home in Gölle. The guest was Géza Wéhner, a professor at the Franz Liszt Music Academy in Budapest and chief organist of the capital's great Dohány Street Synagogue.

He listened attentively as she played and sang a classical Italian song, and afterwards asked, 'Would you be interested in a career in music?'

'More than anything!'

'We'll be holding auditions at the Music Academy soon. Come to Budapest and look me up.'

Vali agreed right away.

But Gizella Rácz was not at all in favour of the move. 'Budapest is so far away, why must you go? Stay here, get married and settle down.' She pleaded with her daughter in the way that she had pleaded with her husband fifteen years earlier, when he was considering whether to take up his music scholarship in Italy. It didn't work the second time. Ferenc, who understood what it meant to have dreams and ambitions, encouraged her to go.

The audition was successful. And so, in September 1932, she boarded the train to Budapest, leaving behind the three prospective suitors from among whom her mother had hoped she would choose a husband, the L-shaped house and the village of Gölle, to which she would afterwards return only in the capacity of honoured visitor – the local girl made good.

Three years later, she stepped on to the stage of the Academy's vast auditorium to receive her diploma from the then Director of the Academy, the renowned composer Ernő Dohnányi. By then she already knew that her real talent lay not in opera or classical concert music, but in a more popular and vibrant musical form of the day – she was a born *chanteuse*. What was more, with her looks she could hope to enter the film world which she found very appealing. And indeed, only a year later, she made her first film. It was called *Spider's Web* and her name appeared on the billboards. Everything was happening so fast, it seemed only minutes before the papers were referring to Vali Rácz as 'Hungary's latest film star'.

From peasant to film star in only two generations. Not bad at all.

★

Géza Wéhner was the first of a long line of influential Jewish figures in the artistic world who were to play decisive roles in shaping Vali's career.

Paul Ábrahám was another. A successful composer of operettas such as *Ball at the Savoy*, he also wrote the scores for several films made at the UFA Studios in Berlin. Vali met him socially and it was through his patronage that, soon after she finished her studies, she received her first singing engagement – to appear nightly for two months at the Negrescó Café, along the famous promenade called the 'Corsó'. This exclusive stretch of riverside in Pest, between the Chain Bridge and the Elizabeth Bridge, boasted some of the capital's grandest hotels: the Carlton, the Bristol, the Hungária and the Ritz, as well as those other haunts of the jet set, the Negrescó and du Barry cafés and the Prince of Wales Bar.

In the summer of 1936 she appeared in a variety show at one of the resorts on Lake Balaton. In the audience was Aladár Roboz, director of the Terézkörúti Theatre in Budapest, famed for its lively revues and one-act comedies. He asked her to join the theatre's permanent company. She accepted, and for the next two years, as one of its few non-Jewish members, she worked with some of the most talented performers of the time.

It was at the Terézkörúti Theatre that she began to extend her growing repertoire to include music quite different from the popular *chansons* with which she was becoming identified. Of less mass appeal, perhaps, but closer to her heart were the classical Magyar poems, by poets such as Endre Ady, Attila József, Ernő Szép and Mihály Babits, which were being set to music by a generation of brilliant composers. A great many of these composers, including Egon Kemény, János Kerekes and Dezső Szenkár (brother of internationally-known conductor Jenő Szenkár), were Jewish. They wrote ballads of haunting beauty, pervaded with a characteristic Magyar melancholy.

Vali found the deeply Magyar music of Kodály and Bartók, too, more satisfying to perform than the popular hits and film songs of the day. They were given lyrics by some of the finest Hungarian poets and writers. And although the record companies were not interested in recording these less commercial songs, that did not deter Vali from consistently including them in her repertoire.

One poet whom Vali virtually made her own was the wild fifteenth-century Frenchman François Villon, whose *Petit Testament* and *Grand Testament* were translated (or rather, recreated in the Hungarian language) by the poet György Faludy, and set to music by Dezső Szenkár. She was the first to perform these

12

songs, singing them in an elegant period-style dress of black taffeta. Her love of Villon came about through another vital Jewish influence in her life: that of Paul Engel, with whom she had her first serious love affair.

Engel was the older brother of the novelist László Dormándi-Engel, who had emigrated to Paris before the war and achieved considerable success there. Paul was a rich landowner who had inherited his family's baroque castle at Dormánd, in central Hungary. Vali met this worldly intellectual with refined literary tastes the year after she graduated from the Academy. She was renting a one-room flat in Pest at the time. He presented her with her own beautifully furnished flat with a panoramic view on Castle Hill, and encouraged her to feel at home in his castle, too. Then, in the summer of 1937, he swept her away on a motoring holiday which changed her life. He showed her the dazzling world which existed beyond the borders of Hungary and Austria. They drove to Italy in his Renault sports car – he showed her Venice, Milan, the art treasures of Florence – then on to Juan les Pins and other high spots of the French Riviera, and Monte Carlo, where Vali first won a lot of money, then lost it all. Set against the backdrop of this carefree, romantic holiday, their affair blossomed and glowed.

Vali would have been interested in marriage, but Engel shrank from it. He had seen his first wife shot and killed by her jealous lover, and he couldn't bring himself to marry again. Neither was he particularly faithful to Vali: in her absence he enjoyed the company of various young starlets. Inevitably, their romance fell apart. But the effect it had on her was lasting and very special.

When the great dramatic actress, Sári Fedák, came to the Terézkörúti Theatre and heard Vali sing, she exclaimed, 'The good Lord himself intended this girl to be a singer!' Fedák never forgot Vali and later, when one of her films required a glamorous *chanteuse*, she made sure the part went to her.

One evening in 1938 the Rónay brothers came to see the show. Ödön Rónay ran both the plush restaurant in the Vigadó building and the Hangli Kioszk which stood in the square before it, facing the Danube. The Hangli was a unique place – a café-restaurant in the shape of a huge glass dome, rather like a conservatory, in the middle of a garden. At night, the view through its walls was spectacular: the bridges glowed, the river sparkled with reflected lights and the Castle dominated the skyline on the other side.

His brother Miklós managed the nearby Belvárosi Coffee House and Grill, a famous establishment, together with his son Egon, who doubtless found this a useful preparation for his later career as Britain's food critic *extraordinaire*.

Ödön realized at once that Vali Rácz would make the perfect nightly entertainer for his Hangli Kioszk. Live music was one of its main attractions and he needed performers of a very high calibre to satisfy the demands of his clientele: regular customers included members of the aristocracy, government ministers, and famous writers, actors and journalists from around the world.

And so began the most significant engagement of Vali's career – her six years as resident *chanteuse* at the Hangli. From ten p.m. to midnight she appeared five times, always in different clothes chosen to suit the mood of the songs she was singing, whether the hits from her own films, wartime songs like *Lili Marlene* or ballads by Villon. Some songs even called for a top hat and tails – the sight of her dressed like that never failed to thrill the audience. The *Pesti Napló* (Diary of Pest) of 7 October 1938, declared that the woman had definite *szekszepil* – sex appeal, in the quaint Hungarianized spelling of the expression. Her success was enormous and she earned three times as much as the biggest stars of the legitimate stage in Budapest. Throughout the season, September to May, she sang every night, except for Christmas Eve and Good Friday.

There were no other popular singers at the time with the combination of qualities she offered: a fine voice, technique and versatility. Because of this, many composers wrote songs specifically for her. She could handle even the more technically difficult numbers with ease, while most of her colleagues, unable to read music, learned their songs laboriously by ear.

But what really made Vali Rácz unique was the appealing blend of contrasts within her persona. She was sleek and

14

worldly, yet she never lost the aura of the countryside. The papers often wrote with amusement about her passion for gardening. There was a simplicity, a natural and wholesome quality about her which was rare in her profession.

One night in 1939, Franz Lehár came to the Hangli, in the company of the brilliant lyricist, Zsolt Harsányi. The sixty-nine-year-old composer was visiting Budapest from his home in Vienna and staying at the Hungária Hotel, a couple of doors away. He was so impressed by Vali's singing that he asked her to call on him the next day. When they met he said he'd like her to sing a piece of music he had written, which had not yet been performed. He would arrange for Harsányi to write the words to it and return to Budapest with it soon.

Some months later he returned, as promised, and at a special event which he invited the press to record, he presented her with the handwritten music of *Ging da nicht eben das glück vorbei?* ('Wasn't it Luck that Just Passed By?') He also tried to persuade her to come to Vienna, claiming to feel thirty years younger in her company. He said he'd like to write an operetta especially for her. That, however, was another matter. The Anschluss had already taken place the previous year, and Austria was now Nazi territory. Vali was not eager to spend time there. They parted.

She sang his song sometimes, though, at the Hangli and at concerts. They never met again but for quite a while kept up a correspondence. Lehár's letters from Vienna were always censored. The envelopes arrived marked *Geöffnet*, 'Opened', and occasionally part of the contents was missing. What could the Nazis have objected to? His last request was for an autographed picture of her.

Sándor Gergely was as instrumental as anyone in moulding Vali's image as a *mondaine*. This exclusive *couturier* had one of the finest salons in the capital. He went to see her one night during her early days at the Hangli and after her performance introduced himself with these words: 'Madam, I do not like your dress.'

'Is that so?' The *chanteuse* was surprised.

'If you will allow me, I'd like to design a dress for you

15

myself – free of charge. All I ask is that, if you are pleased with it, from now on you have all your stage dresses made at my salon.'

It was a deal. The dress that Gergely made for her was superb: a floor-length gown of turquoise crêpe in what they called the 'English style', with short sleeves, collar and dark belt. It caused a sensation when she first sang in it at the Hangli, because it was very different from the usual sort of thing worn then by singers in Budapest. It made her seem like an exotic import from Hollywood, especially with her new swept-up hairstyle and in her high-heeled, open-toed gold shoes. The Ronáy brothers, sitting in the audience that night, gaped at her with open mouths.

Afterwards Gergely dressed her as if she were one of his models, in creations as stunning and flattering as anything to be found in Paris. Decades later, when friends now ageing and in exile reminisced about those years when Vali Rácz reigned at the Hangli, they would often sigh, 'And those dresses, my God, Vali, those glorious dresses that you wore . . .'

In 1941, under the pro-German government of Prime Minister Bárdossy, the punitive Third Jewish Law was passed in Hungary, also known as the Race Protection Law. Sándor Gergely was Jewish, and he didn't share the naïve optimism of most other Hungarian Jews, who convinced themselves that things were bearable, that they wouldn't get worse, and that if they only sat tight, they could weather the storm of Nazism. Gergely felt instinctively that things could, and would get much worse. Since 1940 there had been a series of laws and decrees concerning the Jewish labour service, which was, for the majority of the men conscripted into it, tantamount to a death sentence. In late 1942 he received his labour service call-up papers. He closed down his salon and gave Vali a parting gift of a black velvet dress he had just finished. Soon afterwards he poisoned himself.

His death was a terrible blow to Vali. Her many Jewish friends and associates in the arts were at that time still, by and large, able to carry on with their careers (unless they had been conscripted into the labour service). And she wanted to believe,

16

as they did, that the situation was improving in Hungary.

After all, as early as the spring of 1942, the new prime minister, Miklós Kállay, with Horthy's encouragement, had been trying to extricate Hungary from the Axis camp. Nazi fanaticism was abhorrent to him. Disturbed by the rumours reaching him regarding the true fate of the Jews evacuated from neighbouring countries ostensibly for 'road construction', he would not bow to German demands for *Entjudung* – the de-Jewification of Hungary, refusing even to make Jews wear the yellow star.

The Hungarian government managed to keep secret from the Germans and their sympathizers in Hungary the fact that they were operating a rescue organization, smuggling stranded Allied POWs out of Hungary to the partisans in Yugoslavia whence they continued on their way to the Middle East.

In May 1943, Kállay gave a speech rebutting German pressure. 'Hungary,' he said, 'will never deviate from those precepts of humanity which, in the course of its history, it has always maintained in racial and religious questions.' Quietly, he initiated secret negotiations with the Allies and played for time, hoping to mislead the Germans and steal his vulnerable country away from under the nose of Hitler.

His speech incensed the Führer, who had repeatedly warned Regent Horthy that any country which did not rid itself of its Jewish 'parasites' was doomed to perish. Then, through his spies, he learned about Hungary's attempts to make a separate peace. This he could not allow. Having a friend of the Allies directly on the Reich's eastern border would leave it wide open to attack; his strategy required an Axis buffer zone. And so, less than a year later, in March 1944, he vented the full extent of his fury on what he called 'this Jewish-influenced State'. Kállay was ousted and replaced by a quisling, Döme Sztójay, who was only too willing to comply with the orders of the impatient Nazis. Hence Operation Margarethe.

The concert by Chappy, 'the King of Jazz' due to take place at the Vigadó was not the only thing to be cancelled that Sunday morning. Many things were to come then to an irrevocable end, among them the Hangli Kioszk. Opposite the Vigadó, the great glass dome, too, was deserted. It was closed down that day never to reopen. The Rónays, a Jewish family, were forced into hiding. Bombed the following winter during the Siege of Budapest, there was nothing left of the Hangli after the war but broken glass and rubble.

Three

The phone rang at 47d Budakeszi Avenue one evening early in May. Vali had been spending a lot more time at home since the Occupation as her work had been completely disrupted. With the Hangli closed, many other establishments and activities ceasing and people disappearing in the political maelstrom, she was 'resting', whether she wanted to or not.

She answered the phone and heard Bandi Schreiber's urgent voice at the other end of line.

'Could I come to see you tomorrow?' he asked.

'Yes, of course. What is it, Bandi?'

'I can't speak now.'

They agreed to meet the following morning.

She had known Schreiber since the summer of 1941. He ran the prestigious New York Hotel in the Transylvanian city of Kolozsvár. Soon after the Germans returned northern Transylvania to Hungary in the second Vienna Award in 1940, Schreiber invited Vali to be resident *chanteuse* at the restaurant/bar of his hotel for the following year's summer season, from June to August. That fitted in perfectly with her arrangements at the Hangli, so she gladly accepted.

She had such success at the New York that Schreiber engaged her again for the following summer. Ancient Kolozsvár was not only beautiful, it was also a rich cultural capital, and Vali fell in love with it.

Those two summers were also notable for leading to Vali's first ever aeroplane trips. She became fascinated by flying, having spent an entire return flight from Kolozsvár joking and chatting with the pilots in the cockpit, who were only too happy to explain the control panel to their glamorous passenger. They asked whether she'd be interested in taking flying lessons, and she said yes, of course she would. So it was arranged. Not long afterwards she was taken up in a two-seater by an instructor who did his best to give her the scare of her life. He did loop-the-loops, spins, turns and dives. But she didn't show fear and, luckily, managed not to be sick. On the ground, the amused pilots were wondering if she could take it. When the plane finally landed, they ran over to their 'protegée'. Vali jumped out, a little unsteadily, and said, 'Thanks, it was fun. But I think I'll stick to singing.' They had a good laugh and parted friends.

But all that was in happier days.

What could Bandi be phoning about now? He was a Jew, and although he had a Christian wife, this mitigating factor might no longer be taken into account. Did he need her help?

When Bandi arrived in the morning, he lost no time in revealing his pressing problem to Vali. The situation, he explained, was becoming increasingly dangerous for the Jews of Budapest. Alarming news was reaching the capital from all over the countryside: following the marking of Jews with the yellow star and their forced removal into ghettos, all the signs indicated that mass deportations were about to begin. Although the process had not yet begun in Budapest, panic was spreading among the city's Jews. Desperately, they were trying to obtain forged identity papers from the secret Zionist resistance, or protective certificates from the consulates of the neutral countries, the Red Cross and the Papal Nuncio. But public opinion had been poisoned by the years of rabid and systematic propaganda by the extreme-Right minority in Hungary. And now Jews were being shunned by their Gentile friends and neighbours, and those living with false Christian papers were being denounced. Humane Gentiles trying to help them were branded as traitors.

'I am turning to you, Vali,' he said, 'because I know I can trust you, I know what kind of person you are. I need help. Not for myself – I think I am safe for the moment at my flat in Pest – but for others. In recent days my cousin, Jenő Mandel, and his wife were denounced. They are desperately trying to find some place to hide until all this is over. Could you take them in? The police would not think of suspecting you.'

Vali was aware of the potential perils of such an undertaking, but her reply gave Bandi hope. 'Of course if I can help you, I will. But I need a little time to think it through. Will you contact me in a day or two?'

As soon as Bandi left, she phoned various places and eventually reached the one person she knew she must talk to, and quickly – Paul Barabás. For several years he had been her close friend and confidant, acting almost as a personal manager, and she had implicit faith in his judgement. He was the kind of friend you could entrust your life to, which was precisely what she now proceeded to do.

To the Hungarian public, Vali was the star and Barabás was the highly successful writer in whose films and plays she so frequently appeared. But in private, their relationship was more complex than that.

They met in 1938 at that famous haunt of writers and journalists, the Hullamosó ('Corpse-Washer') pub, so called because it was next door to the part of the Rókus Hospital where they cleaned up the corpses and the men who cleaned them often drank there. Barabás was a *habitué*; Vali was sometimes invited there by newspapermen and critics. He had recently returned from Berlin, where his latest film was being shot at the UFA Studios, and he had interesting stories to tell about life in the Third Reich. They liked each other at once.

As their friendship grew, Barabás found himself utterly in love with the newly-installed singer of the Hangli Kioszk. And as far as he was concerned, the fact that he already had a wife and son posed no obstacle at all. He simply omitted to tell her about them. They lived conveniently out of the way on the outskirts of Budapest, while he lived mainly in a flat on Rose Hill, conveniently near to Budakeszi Avenue. The flat was in the villa of the actress, Klári Tolnay, who made several films with Vali.

21

Vali and Barabás began an intense affair. She even considered marriage. But, inevitably, it wasn't long before she found out about his family. And when she did, she erupted. (To say that Vali Rácz had an 'artistic temperament' is something of an understatement.) Although she didn't actually end the affair, she didn't take the physical side of their relationship too seriously after that, having other lovers besides him. But Barabás was so passionately devoted and loyal to Vali that he accepted the relationship on whatever terms she cared to dictate. And he did all he could to promote her career, writing parts for her in nearly all of his films and plays. She was his adored 'Valikó'.

Now she needed his advice. Could she take in the Mandels? Would it be safe? Paul would know what to do.

Barabás, under the cover of his enthusiasm for working in Berlin, was an ardent anti-Nazi. In the weeks following the Occupation he allied himself with the growing resistance movement in Hungary, writing and printing anti-Nazi pamphlets which were secretly distributed among the population of Budapest.

He called on Vali that evening. She confided in him, and together they worked out the logistics of a possible plan. The Mandels could sleep in the basement and stay within the house at all times, but what would happen in the (unlikely) event of a Gestapo raid? They went through the house slowly, room by room. There would have to be a hiding place in which they could conceal themselves while the house was being searched.

Although the house was beautifully furnished, it was modest in size. It had two floors, plus the basement. On the ground floor there was a central reception room, where Vali kept the baby grand, and a book-lined dining area with French doors leading to the garden. To the right of the entrance hall was a small front bedroom used by the housekeeper. To the left of it was a lavatory, and a little further along, the kitchen and the larder, from which a flight of stairs led down to the basement.

The basement ran the length of the house and had three inter-connecting rooms. As it was partially above ground level, the rooms had windows facing the large back garden. Two of

22

the rooms had been designed as servants' quarters (although unoccupied now, as Vali no longer had a maid) and the third contained a boiler and was used for storage.

From a corner in the rear of the reception room a staircase led up to the first floor. This had two further bedrooms, one of which was Vali's, and a bathroom. The bedrooms opened on to a balcony, which was above the housekeeper's room and dining area. There was a good view from the balcony of tree-lined Budakeszi Avenue and, beyond it, the hills of Buda. Vali had often been photographed there for the arts and entertainment magazines.

It was in Vali's bedroom that Barabás hit upon a brilliant idea. When she was having the house built six years earlier, she wanted her bedroom to have a large built-in wardrobe to accommodate her stage clothes and evening gowns. The bedroom was next to the staircase, and so the architect cleverly decided to build the wardrobe into the adjoining wall and extend it right back into the space above the staircase. This gave the wardrobe an unexpected depth, while maintaining the ordinary appearance of the staircase.

Barabás's idea was to divide the wardrobe in half by putting a false wall into the middle of it. This would reduce it to a conventional size, and at the same time create a secret compartment behind it. As this secret compartment was directly over the staircase, it sloped sharply on one side, as it followed the line of the ceiling above the stairs.

The false wall would have to swing outwards easily, like a door, to allow for speedy entry into the secret compartment, and the Mandels would need to be able to lock it tightly into position again from the inside. It must be made to match the other walls of the room, with the same slender wooden edging.

It was an ingenious scheme. And almost foolproof . . . almost, because there was one slight drawback. Should anyone knock on the false wall, it would naturally sound hollow. It would not be difficult then to deduce that there was some kind of concealed space behind it, extending over the stairs. But neither Barabás nor Vali were unduly worried. If the wardrobe looked absolutely right it would not arouse suspicion.

They talked about Zsóka, the housekeeper and cook. She was a dark-haired, swarthy woman in her early forties, of Transylvanian peasant stock. Could she be trusted? Might she perhaps be tempted to betray the Jews for personal gain? Vali considered this carefully. Zsóka had been working for her and living at the house for a year and a half. She was good-natured enough, if not too bright, and always did what was expected of her. There was no reason to doubt her loyalty.

She was Vali's sole employee since the departure of Boriska, the young Jewish secretary whom Vali had brought back with her from Kolozsvár after her second engagement there in the summer of 1942. Boriska, who had lived at the house, left after the Occupation to take up a less conspicuous position in Pest. As Vali's secretary, she accompanied the singer wherever she went and led a high-profile existence. This was no longer desirable after the Germans took over.

So, besides Zsóka, the only other occupant of the house was Juliska, a beautiful young Komondor – the traditional white-haired sheepdog from the lowlands of Hungary. Vali had recently received her as a gift from a breeder. She slept in a kennel in the back garden and was swiftly becoming a good watchdog.

Barabás told Vali that he would take care of everything. He had a trustworthy friend who was skilled in carpentry and would carry out the necessary work at once.

'Everything will be fine,' he assured her, in parting. 'You're doing the right thing, Valikó.'

*

Jenő and Szerén Mandel were a quiet middle-aged couple who owned a flourishing business in Budapest. The five stores in the Hungária Gumi Textil chain specialized in products made with rubber, such as medical corsets and elastic stockings. Of course, as soon as the Nazis arrived the business was closed down and the Mandels were stigmatized. They were consoled by the knowledge that their son, who had emigrated some years earlier to South America, was safe from the upheavals and tragedies of the war.

24

As soon as they arrived, Vali discussed certain essential precautions with them – they could go outside to the garden for fresh air only after dark; they must stay away from the front windows; and in the event of friends or visitors coming to the house, they were to remain silently in the basement until the visitors were gone. No one must discover their presence.

The Mandels were Orthodox, and their unswerving faith saved them from despondency. Despite their vast religious and cultural differences, Vali and the Mandels understood each other very well. She made things as comfortable as possible for them in one of the basement rooms, where, each Friday evening, they lit candles and celebrated Sabbath.

Meanwhile, throughout the Hungarian countryside, Eichmann was eradicating in record time one of the most prosperous and thriving Jewish communities in Europe, hoping to impress Hitler and his immediate boss, Chief of Police and Minister of the Interior, Heinrich Himmler. By now, as a result of years of experience in the systematic application of science to mass murder, his technique had been perfected. The 'yellow star decree' was followed by the formation of a Jewish Council to lull the Jews into a false security and acquiescence, then all their assets would be expropriated, they would be herded into ghettos, and from there put on to the assembly line for murder – the trains to Auschwitz. Beginning on 14 May, 12,000 Jews were deported daily. The country had been divided into six zones which were being, one by one, emptied of Jews. Budapest was designated the sixth and final zone for clearance.

Eichmann was in a hurry. The Reich was in urgent need of slave labour to aid the war effort. Those who were temporarily reprieved from the gas chambers would be put to work in various labour camps. Besides, he was an extremely ambitious man, with a craving for personal glory. Even at this late stage of the war, with the Germans in constant retreat, he was determined to finish his job and whisk away to their doom the last remaining Jews of Europe.

Assisting Eichmann in his task were the *Sonderkommando*, his team of specialists; his two closest collaborators in the Hungarian quisling government, László Baky and László Endre

– Interior Ministry state secretaries in charge of the Jewish question; and the bloodthirsty forces of the Hungarian gendarmerie, who seemed intent on surpassing even the SS in their vicious treatment of the Jews. It was all being overseen by Edmund Veesenmayer, Hitler's tireless Plenipotentiary in Hungary, who sent frequent detailed progress reports to von Ribbentrop at the Foreign Office in Berlin.

Eichmann made his headquarters on top of Swabian Hill, one of the wooded hills in Buda, from which he had a magnificent, eagle's-eye view of the capital. There, in the splendid seclusion of the Hotel Majestic, commandeered for his purposes, he reigned over the conquered city of Budapest.

Chief among his hirelings was Péter Hain, head of the Hungarian Secret Police, who also ensconced himself at the Majestic. His job was to track down all enemies of the Reich at large in the capital – Jews in hiding, army deserters, members of the resistance – and wring confessions out of them through torture.

Hain had another interest, too. Eagerly he seized a quantity of priceless art treasures which had been stored by their Jewish owners in cellars for protection against air raids. All Jewish valuables were deemed rightful spoils by the Sztójay government, but Eichmann naturally demanded part of the booty for himself and his commando. That summer Hain organized a fabulous display of these confiscated treasures at the Majestic: paintings by Rembrandt, Rubens, Van Dyck and other old masters, antique tapestries, Persian carpets, silver, gold and jewels. He exploited it fully for anti-Jewish propaganda in the press. Afterwards, he was to arouse the ire of both the Nazis and their collaborators when they realized that he had embezzled sixty million pengős' worth of gold and jewellery while in possession of the treasures. In the end, Eichmann had the bulk of these valuables carted off to Germany in military trucks and trains.

Another important figure on the scene was Obersturmbahnführer Kurt Becher, Himmler's personal representative and economic emissary, who had arrived with the occupation forces in March. He arranged an extraordinary deal on behalf of his superior. He acquired for the SS the most lucrative and vital industrial enterprise in Hungary: the Manfred Weiss Works in Csepel, an island on the Danube on the southern outskirts of Budapest. Its vast munitions factory was essential for Germany's war effort.

In exchange for the transferal of ownership for a twenty-five-year period to the SS, the wealthy industrialist families of Weiss, Chorin and Kornfeld, who owned the works, would be allowed to leave Hungary before the deportations began. And so, that spring, forty-five members of those families were driven to Vienna and afterwards flown to Lisbon. One member of each family, however, had to remain in Vienna as a hostage, to prevent the others from participating in anti-Nazi activities abroad.

★

At the end of May, Vali received an anxious call from her friend Margit Herzog, asking her to come to her flat in Buda. She feared the worst. The Herzogs were a large, wealthy Jewish family with a great deal to lose.

Margit's late father, Ignác, was a prominent landowner and an industrialist. He founded the family fortune, which included a 600-hectare estate at Losonc, in southern Slovakia, with livestock farms and alcohol refineries, and the vast Csengőd vineyards, producing some of Hungary's best known wine. The family residence in Budapest was on Andrássy Avenue, the grandest boulevard in the city, next door to the home of Hungary's foremost aristocratic family, the Széchenyis.

Vali first met the family through Sándor, Margit's brother and the eldest of five siblings, in the late 1930s. He was her suitor – a kind, genial man who ran the family's refineries. He enjoyed vacationing at fashionable resorts on the Adriatic coast, and liked the company of theatre and film people. He proposed marriage. Although Vali was very fond of him, she declined.

Sándor spent much of his time in Losonc, but they saw each other when he came to Budapest. And Vali maintained a friendship with Margit, a bright, lively companion and superb sportswoman. Throughout the 1920s and 1930s she had won

27

a series of trophies at tennis competitions in Hungary, Czechoslovakia, France and Italy. But now she had settled down, and
was the mother of two children – a fourteen-year-old daughter,
Marietta, by her first husband, and five-year-old Péter by her
second.

Dezső, her second husband, had already suffered terribly
during his year and a half in the labour service. His unit had
been posted to the Eastern Front in the spring of '42. One day
he and a few others were cooking potatoes over an open fire – it
was in Russia, and the Front was very near – when they were
accused of trying to 'signal' their position to the enemy. They
were hanged from posts by their hands, which were tied
together with cord. For many hours the labour servicemen
were left hanging. When they passed out from the pain, they
were doused with water. Eventually they were taken down.

The following year, his unit dismantled, Desző was back in
Budapest. He showed his wife the appalling scars on his wrists.
His term of duty in the labour service had ended, but he feared
that he might be called up once more. He vowed that he would
assume a false identity rather than go through that hell again.

The Herzogs were among the first people Vali thought of
when the Germans occupied the country. No one in the family
had thought of taking steps to forestall the dangers of a Nazi
take-over. Like many other Jews, wealthy and otherwise, they
wanted to believe that, despite the passing political traumas, the
traditionally tolerant aristocracy/gentry leadership of Hungary
would, in the end, protect them. Also, they were strongly
bound to their land and their fortune. They simply couldn't
abandon it. It was to be a fatal mistake.

Within days of the Occcupation, Vali took the train to
Losonc. She got into a taxi at the small local station and
instructed the driver to take her to the Herzog estate. He
seemed interested and casually inquired about the nature of her
visit. But Vali told him little.

She stayed that night with Sándor, Margit, another brother
and their widowed mother. For hours they talked about the
political situation and speculated on the course of the war and
on their own precarious position. Even then Sándor was quietly

reassuring. And the following morning, he accompanied her to the railway station where they said a tender farewell.

Vali was about to board the train when two men appeared at either side of her, grabbed her arms and took her to a room in the station building. They searched her small overnight case but, finding little else besides a nightgown, slippers and some make-up, after a few gruff words they told her she could leave. It was apparent that the plainclothesmen had been waiting for her. Anyone associating with the Herzog family was suspect, and they'd been tipped off, probably by the taxi driver who'd taken her there. They were disappointed, though, if they'd expected to find incriminating letters or documents.

Now, as she sat with Margit in the drawing room of her flat, Vali asked whether there was any news about Sándor and the others.

'They've been deported,' said Margit. 'Within the last few days, I received a mysterious postcard from my brother Feri. The message read: "I have arrived, I am well." '

'Where was the card from?'

'It was postmarked "Waldsee". I've never heard of it.'

As a Jew she was no longer permitted to travel, so she couldn't get to Losonc. And their telephone there had been disconnected. She was particularly concerned about her elderly mother, about whom there had been no word.

She had been able to keep in touch only with her brother Imre, who lived in another part of Budapest. He belonged to the one élite group of Jews who were so highly regarded, even by the post-Occupation regime, that they were still able to go about their business unmolested: the decorated heroes of World War I. Imre was nineteen when, in 1915, as a Hussar with the 15th Nyiregyházi Regiment, he was sent to the Russian Front. He was decorated for engaging in valiant hand-to-hand combat, during which he lost an arm. After the war the handsome young hero, honourably discharged from the army, developed a reputation in Budapest as a dashing and debonair man-about-town. He was often to be seen strolling along elegant Váci Street, the empty sleeve of his jacket neatly tucked into his pocket. 'One-armed Imre', they dubbed him.

29

Now Margit came to the point of their meeting. Her husband had been working out a plan to save them from the mass deportations from Budapest which he knew would soon begin. He had obtained a false Christian identity for himself – Desző Keleti became 'József Papp' – with which he would attempt to live openly. He had arranged for friends of his, a married couple who were members of the underground Communist movement, to take in their son Péter, also with a false identity. But Margit and his step-daughter Marietta would have to go into hiding. And that was where Vali came in.

This time she didn't need to think it over. She told Margit about the Mandels, and said that there was room for two more at the villa. She described the wardrobe with its false wall. The secret compartment was large enough to conceal them all, in an emergency.

It was having to part from her son which most upset Margit.

'Where is Péter now?' asked Vali, who had never met the child.

'I sent him out for a walk with the nanny, just before you came. I didn't want him to see you, to be able to recognize you. Who knows? If the Gestapo should find him . . . it's as well to take every precaution, and the less he knows the better.'

When all the arrangements were ready, the family made its escape. It was an auspicious day, that Tuesday that Margit and Marietta moved into the villa: 6 June 1944, D-Day. At long last the Allies had landed in Normandy. Surely the Germans would soon be defeated now that the Americans had arrived. The very name 'America' was to most Hungarians synonymous with hope. In a state of elation, they all stood around the radio beside the big tiled stove in the sitting room, listening to the BBC.

They had no idea that, for the people of Budapest, the worst was yet to come. And that it would be more horrifying and more tragic than anything they had imagined.

Four

Vali placed the folder down on the table before the functionary who had set up office in the radio-station building. The dour young man opened the folder and carefully examined each document. They were birth certificates, extending back for three generations. They were all in order – not a Jew among them.

He put the documents away. With a disdainful smile, he handed the folder back. 'You're lucky,' he said. No one was permitted to take part in a broadcast without first establishing their racial acceptability.

Vali struggled to contain her ire. She'd been one of the radio's most popular singers for a decade, ever since her erstwhile violin teacher at the Academy, Tivadar Ország, had given her the personal recommendation to radio producers which began her long and fruitful association with that medium. (He despaired of her violin playing, but was convinced she would find fame as a singer.)

The public could hear Vali sing that day. But it was to be a rare occurrence that summer, for with the turbulent political atmosphere and the secret activities at the villa, her career was no longer the pivotal feature of her life. She withdrew as much as possible into her own domain at 47d Budakeszi Avenue, discouraging even friends from visiting. Each visit brought with it the risk of exposure for the Jews. And yet, she couldn't seal herself away completely, as that might arouse suspicion. Hence her acceptance of the invitation to appear that day on radio.

Obtaining food had become a constant worry. The war was creating ever greater shortages. And now there were four extra people to feed. Vali's good fortune during the war had been the occasional food parcels sent up from Gölle by her parents. They posted large baskets filled with salamis, smoked hams and sausages, potatoes, flour and other provisions becoming scarce in the capital. Sometimes a visiting acquaintance from the village would deliver the hamper to her. But this might not be able to continue for long; trains and postal services were growing erratic.

So Vali concerned herself mainly with the day-to-day logistics of running her extended household. Nothing could have been more different from the previous years of the war, when her work schedule was so exhausting and relentless that admiring newspapermen were sometimes given to little leaps of hyperbole. 'Vali Rácz is to give her 6,000th consecutive singing performance at the Vigadó this Sunday night,' one of them enthused in January 1944. And another one assembled the following statistics regarding her career: 'One hundred composers have between them written 240 songs for her, which she has sung on about 10,000 occasions, on café podiums, in concerts and on the radio. Her renditions of other *chansons* have resounded 50,000 times before live audiences . . .'

If somewhat far-fetched, such pieces in the press reflected the widely accepted and accurate view of Vali as one of the hardest-working and most dedicated performers in the country. During the day she made films – up to four a year – and at night she put in five appearances at the Hangli. She made records. And in between all of this were the concerts – she sang in scores of them, all over the country.

Besides the usual concerts which were purely for entertainment, there were many charity concerts, often organized by the Hungarian Red Cross. They raised money for hospitals for wounded soldiers, war orphans and war widows. There were gala concerts and memorial concerts, such as the one given in memory of István Horthy, the Regent's son, who died when his plane crashed in dubious circumstances on the Eastern Front in August 1942. The proceeds from it were given to a residential school for war orphans at Lake Balaton.

Various organizations, trade unions and even factories gave charity concerts, and often solicited Vali's participation. She never refused. She sang for the railwaymen's union, the employees of a machine-making factory and an aeroplane-parts factory, the National Association of Hungarian Students . . .

And then there were the so-called 'request concerts' for the Hungarian troops, often broadcast live to the Front. The Second Hungarian Army was mobilized early in 1942, and throughout 1942 and 1943 she sang at these morale-boosting events. She deliberately chose songs which, rather than glorifying the war and whipping up aggression, aimed at comforting the soldiers and reassuring them that one day it would all be over. According to the monthly *Illustrated Army Camp News*, which interviewed her for its October 1942 issue, Vali was the troops' favourite and received more letters from the Front than anyone else. This was how they ended their interview with her:

'Are you happy and fulfilled?' we ask.
'I will be when they are all back home again,' she replies, pointing to the bundles of letters from the Front.
To all her fans and admirers she sends her wishes for their good health, good humour and courage . . . we convey this message, until the time when her fans on the Front can once again hear her in person.

For most of them, that time never came. The Second Hungarian Army fighting with the Wehrmacht on the Eastern Front was decimated during the winter of 1942–3, when the Russians finally made their decisive breakthrough at the River Don. Out of 200,000 soldiers, 140,000 were killed. Stationed with them were 50,000 brutally treated Jewish labour-servicemen (including Margit Herzog's husband), who were used for clearing minefields, building roads, trenches and fortifications and shifting military stores and ammunition. During the bitter retreat, 42,000 of them died.

This defeat began the gradual disintegration of the Hungarian army, from which, the following year, there was to be widespread desertion, even at senior-officer level. It was becoming clear that Hungary's alignment with Nazi Germany had been a monumental and ruinous mistake.

Its seeds were sown much earlier, in 1932, with the appointment of the country's first virulent anti-Semitic and pro-Nazi prime minister, Gyula Gömbös. He shattered at once the moderate climate created under Count István Bethlen's regime. From 1921 to 1931, Bethlen, a member of the old conservative/aristocratic ruling class which flourished before the First World War, did a great deal to restore economic stability to his truncated nation. Far from wishing to persecute the Jews, he realized that their industrial, commercial and financial cooperation was vital in order to secure that stability.

But his government was unable to control the far-Right radical groups, such as the Association of Awakening Magyars, which forged links with the infant Nazi Party in Germany. Bethlen's regime came to an end as a result of the economic crisis of 1929–30 and the onset of the Depression, which brought financial disaster to Hungary. This paved the way for Gömbös, who came to power at virtually the same time as his friend and ally, Adolf Hitler. During his four-year regime, Gömbös established a far-Right power base in Hungary, which made it possible for the Nazis to penetrate and subvert every aspect of the country's life.

Under Gömbös, an anti-Semitic propaganda campaign was launched. Much was made of the dominant role played by Jews in the short-lived but terroristic Communist regime of Béla Kun in 1919, which sprang up out of the chaos and instability following the Habsburg Empire's demise. While it was true that Kun and eighteen of the twenty-nine members of his Revolutionary Ruling Council were Jewish, the propaganda omitted two important facts: first, that Kun and his men did not represent the Jewish community at all, they regarded themselves merely as Communist revolutionaries; and second, that the Jews as a whole were as much against Kun as anyone – as businessmen and capitalists, they had everything to lose under a Communist regime. But, to serve their ends, the extreme-Rightists branded all Jews as Bolsheviks and anti-patriotic

34

radicals. And in the minds of the common people, after years of indoctrination, the associations began to stick.

Gömbös abandoned, too, Bethlen's belief in the Western democracies and the League of Nations as Hungary's best hope for reversing some of the injustices of the Treaty of Trianon, whereby seventy-one per cent of its territory and sixty-four per cent of its population went to the 'successor states' – Czechoslovakia, Rumania, Yugoslavia and Austria. Gömbös believed that Hungary's revanchist aims would be best served by a close alliance with Germany, another nation which had lost its empire after the First World War – the Hohenzollern monarchy. And Hitler did, of course, sympathize. What the short-sighted prime minister didn't realize was that there would be a tremendous price to pay for German support: the eventual loss of Hungarian sovereignty.

The Jews became an easy scapegoat for Hungary's ills. As the other minorities had been largely absorbed into the successor states, the country changed from being polyglot to being homogeneous. The Jews were the only sizeable minority left, and this made them an obvious target. During the days of the Empire, the assimilation of the Jews was encouraged, and, except for the Orthodox community, the Jews were eager to become 'Magyarized', to ensure their future security and prosperity in Hungary. And many of them outdid even the Magyars in their national chauvinism. But all this changed after the Kun revolution and Trianon, when the Jews began to be isolated and ostracized.

Admiral Nicholas Horthy rode into Budapest on his famous white stallion in November 1919, and from then on he held the reins not only of his horse but of his country. It was his complex personality which was to determine Hungary's destiny for the following two and a half decades.

As Commander-in-Chief of the Adriatic Fleet, Horthy had been a powerful man under the Habsburgs. And now, leading a new national army, he quickly mopped up both the Communist revolutionaries and the Rumanians, who had opportunistically marched into the chaos of Hungary. The following year he was appointed Regent for a monarch, Charles IV, who was then barred from the throne.

Horthy had a schizophrenic attitude towards the Jews. Married to a half-Jewish woman himself, he was nevertheless a self-proclaimed anti-Semite. For the first year of his rule, he let his army get away with its lawless and brutal 'White Terror' – the anti-Jewish backlash after the 'Red Terror' of Kun's Communist revolution. He welcomed the purge of 'radical elements'.

But Horthy was not one to lump together the different communities within the Jewish population. He disliked the Orthodox and Hasidic Jews, who lived mainly in the provinces, those who had emigrated to Hungary from Galicia and other neighbouring territories, and those with Communist sympathies. He was quite happy to see the back of them. But he made a completely separate case for those Jews who, he felt, had contributed to the wealth and welfare of the nation, the assimilated 'Neologs'. Industrialists, bankers, financiers, political advisers, university professors and scientists – these leading, influential Jews he considered not only of great value, but to be as undeniably 'Magyar' as he was himself. Many of them had married into the aristocracy or been given titles themselves. These were 'his Jews', and he defended them with an ardent paternalism.

And so he spent his twenty-five years in power vacillating – at times appointing moderate and humane prime ministers who defied the extreme-Right, at times appointing rabid pro-Nazis and at times merely weak appeasers. He never really understod where his own anti-Semitism began and ended, or just how much leeway the Germans would give him. He was not a dictator, merely an old-fashioned semi-feudal lord who tried to walk a tightrope but inevitably fell.

Béla Imrédy, a former President of the National Bank of Hungary and prime minister from 1938–9, introduced the first two Jewish laws, which greatly reduced the proportion of Jews allowed to participate in the economic and professional life of Hungary. He curried favour with Hitler and allowed the Arrow Cross Party, Hungary's equivalent to the Nazis, to grow unchecked. For this, Horthy forced him to resign. (Although the ostensible reason was the Jewish ancestor he was revealed to have had after an investigation into his background.)

He was succeeded by Count Paul Teleki. A staunch Anglophile, Teleki loathed and feared the Germans. Although an anti-Semite of the old conservative/aristocratic school, he was scholarly, refined and religious. He detested the vulgar and vicious anti-Semitism of the Arrow Cross rabble.

When war was declared, Teleki tried to alter Hungary's political orientation and improve Anglo-Hungarian relations but the country's geopolitical position made this impossible. Throughout the thirties Hungary had grown increasingly indebted to Germany and dependent on it economically. And now Britain viewed the Reich's small and weak neighbour as already lost to the Axis. In November 1940 Hungary was compelled to join the Tripartite Pact between Germany, Italy and Japan, making it impossible later for Hungary not to fight on the Axis side.

By the spring of 1941 German external and internal pressure was so great that Horthy had no choice but to approve Hungary's participation in the Axis invasion of Yugoslavia, a country with which it had not long before signed a non-aggression pact. (As a reward, Hitler gave back to Hungary some of its former Serbian territories.) Immediately after this betrayal, Teleki shot himself in protest, leaving a suicide letter addressed to Horthy.

László Bárdossy, his successor, carried through to its inevitable end what the invasion of Yugoslavia had begun: in June 1941, five days after Germany attacked Russia, Hungary, too, declared war on the 'giant of the East'. And to complete the madness, in December of that year it declared war on the United States as well.

There was an amusing story going around Washington at the time. According to this story, when Bárdossy sent his declaration of war, Secretary of State Cordell Hull went to see President Roosevelt in the White House. Their conversation went something like this:

Hull: Mr President, Hungary has just declared war on us.

Roosevelt: You don't say! And where is this Hungary?
Hull: It is a little kingdom on the Danube.
Roosevelt: A kingdom? Who's the king?
Hull: Hungary hasn't got a king. The country is run by an admiral.
Roosevelt: An admiral? Where is his fleet?
Hull: He has no fleet. Only an army.
Roosevelt: Where is his army, and who's it fighting against?
Hull: It's in Russia, fighting against the Russians.
Roosevelt: Why?
Hull: It wants to expand its territories.
Roosevelt: It wants Russian territories?
Hull: No, not at all. It wants Czechoslovakian and Rumanian territories.
Roosevelt: Then why isn't Hungary fighting against the Czechs and Rumanians?
Hull: Oh, it can't do that, Mr President. They are its allies.

★

Summer arrived in Budapest, and with it the process of *Entjudung* in the city began in earnest. On 24 June some 150,000 Jews were forced to move into buildings marked with a yellow star. Next stop: Auschwitz.

Throughout the rest of the country, in zones one to five, the deportations were being carried out like clockwork. They were scheduled for completion on 9 July. The date set for the commencement of deportations in Budapest – zone six – was 10 July.

By the first week of July, 600,000 Hungarian Jews had been annihilated within one and a half months. Winston Churchill later described the barbarity and speed with which the 'final solution of the Jewish question' was implemented in Hungary as 'probably the greatest and most horrible crime ever committed in the whole history of the world'.

Now Budapest had the last sizeable body of Jews left alive in Nazi-dominated Europe.

But then something extraordinary happened, which was, for Budapest's Jewry, nothing short of a miracle. On 9 July, the very day before the deportations were to begin, Horthy drew the line at last. He ordered them to be stopped. Eichmann was furious.

Horthy's motivation was manifold. It was true that the capital contained many of 'his Jews' and he was genuinely concerned about shielding them. And by now he'd had more than enough of Hitler's Final Solution. But it was also important for him to be seen to be taking a humanitarian stance. He was desperately trying to align himself with the Allies. He didn't want, after the war, to be lumped together with the Nazis. And then there was the Joel Brand case, which had put the murder of Hungary's Jews into the international limelight and was generating protests from all over the world. The pressure on Horthy to take action was suddenly very great.

Joel Brand and his boss, Rezső Kasztner, worked for the Jewish Rescue Committee, a semi-illegal Zionist organization which had been actively involved in helping the Jews of Europe escape deportation since 1942. In May 1944, when Eichmann launched his deportation campaign in Hungary, he summoned the Committee and put a proposal to them: if they could obtain for Germany 10,000 winterized trucks to be used on the Eastern Front, he would in return let the Jews of Hungary go free. The idea of selling Jews for vital *matériel* appealed to this former salesman.

The Committee agreed at once. However, Eichmann promptly broke his promise to delay deportations for a fortnight while the deal was being negotiated. Meanwhile Brand was sent to neutral Istanbul to start negotiations with the international Jewish agencies and the British and American governments. But he was lured by the suspicious British to Cairo, and then detained by them until the end of the war.

Of course the mission was hopeless from the start – neither the US nor Britain would countenance for one moment aiding the Germans in their war effort, or even (as Brand suggested) pretending to do so in order to win time for the Jews. For the Allies, rescuing Jews had never been a priority. (Apart from anything else, what would they do with them all?)

Eichmann was rather relieved at the failure of the scheme,

which had, in any case, been Himmler's idea, not his own. He much preferred to see the rapid resolution of the Jewish problem: that was of even more importance to him than Germany's struggle to win the war.

But the tragic futility of the famous 'trucks for lives' mission did have one positive outcome: the publicity it received and the outcry it caused contributed to Horthy's decision to call a halt. And so the Jews of Budapest, at least for the time being, had been saved, after all.

Eichmann was not to be easily outmanoeuvred. Shortly after Horthy announced the cancellation, he and his henchman, László Baky, attempted to deport the 1,500 prominent Jews interned in the Kistarcsa camp outside Budapest. He packed them on to a train bound for Auschwitz. But Horthy, warned at the last moment by a horrified Jewish Council, ordered the train to be turned back at Hatvan Station. A few days later Eichmann devised a clever ploy to hoodwink both the Jewish Council and Horthy and deport the internees without their knowledge. He succeeded. He also set a new date for the deportations in Budapest: 5 August. It had become a battle of wills.

It was at this time that Vali Rácz accepted responsibility for one more of the city's persecuted Jews. Szerén Mandel's sister, Ilona, was already in hiding in Pest but knew she was in imminent danger of exposure. She had to make a move.

At twenty-five years old, Ilona was young enough to be Szerén's daughter. Szerén was forty-five, the eldest of twelve siblings; Ilona was the second youngest. She was the manageress of one of the Mandels' stores. Her husband, like most other able-bodied Jewish men at that time, was serving in a labour battalion. She was on her own. Like Szerén and Jenő before her, she sought the help of Bandi Schreiber. And Bandi advised her to go to Vali.

It was getting rather crowded at the house, though, and the more fugitives there were, the more dangerous it was for them all. So Vali thought of another solution for Ilona. She would take the attractive young woman down to Gölle to stay with her parents. There, in the undisturbed peace of the old L-shaped house, she could take shelter from the perils of the war until it was all over.

Vali made arrangements for the two of them to travel by train down to Attala-Csoma, the nearest station to Gölle. The four-hour journey was not without its perils. Ilona would naturally carry false papers, but if they aroused suspicion, or if someone recognized and betrayed her, it would mean the end for both of them.

Ilona travelled under the guise of Vali's 'secretary'. Her papers were approved and, as Vali was such a favoured VIP, neither of them were unduly questioned or scrutinized. Everything went smoothly. At the station they were met by the Rácz family coachman, who drove them home in their black horse-drawn carriage.

Ferenc and Gizella Rácz knew nothing of what had been going on at 47d Budakeszi Avenue. Vali had kept it from them not only because it was safer that way, but because she knew it would cause them anxiety. But now she explained about the Mandels and the Herzogs, and the round-up of the Jews in Budapest.

The Ráczes had news for their daughter, too – tragic news regarding Gölle. No village was too small or too remote to escape the net the Nazis had cast to catch the Jews. And at the end of June, when it was the turn of the Dunántúl to be purged, they had come to take the two Wachsman sisters away.

They were the daughters of the late Dr Wachsman, who had for many years been the Ráczes' family doctor. Vali had known him since she was a small child. When she split her lip once during a fall it was Dr Wachsman who put stitches in it. She knew his daughters well, too – Olga and Elza. They never married, but earned their modest living by selling their handiwork – embroidered handkerchiefs and tablecloths. They also did mending and sewing for the people of the village, and sometimes as a child Vali was sent by her mother to the Wachsman sisters with a bundle of linen to be mended. After their father died, they continued to live in his house. That house and that little village were the only home they knew, and they were an integral part of the community. Everyone liked them for their kindness; they never harmed a living thing.

41

But one day the gendarmes stopped at the Wachsman house and ordered the two gentle sisters to get ready to leave. They were allowed to take one small bundle of personal belongings each, then they were put on to a horse-drawn cart and driven out of the village to the entrainment centre and their deaths.

Gölle's only other Jew was taken away with them – Gizella Weiss, another elderly spinster, known locally as 'Sad Gizella'. Unlike Olga and Elza, she was shy and reclusive, rarely speaking to anyone. Her father had once owned a shop in the village. Now she was alone in the world, without relatives or friends. She survived by buying eggs from the peasants and selling them at a small profit to the Jews of other nearby villages. No matter how poor she was, she would accept no charity from her neighbours.

When the gendarmes came for her at her house across the road from the church, she clung to the railings and cried, 'Don't take me! I'm Magyar, too!' so loudly that several villagers came out to see what was going on. The gendarmes beat her hands until she let go. Still weeping, she covered her face with her shawl as she was put on to the cart. There was a rumour later that, as the cart crossed the bridge over a nearby river, Sad Gizella killed herself by jumping into the water. But no one ever knew this for certain. They only knew that she never came back again.

Vali spent a few days in Gölle, helping Ilona to settle in. It was agreed that she should be seen by no one, staying in the house at all times and avoiding all visitors. Although the respected, devout headmaster and his wife were above suspicion, those were treacherous times. The minds of many people had been poisoned and one had to be very careful, even with close friends and neighbours. In a village where everyone knew everyone else's business, it was not so simple to keep secret the presence of a fugitive. And, to make things worse, there was a malicious pro-Nazi gendarme stationed in Gölle who was keeping a sharp eye on things. But the Ráczes made Ilona feel welcome and, in return, she offered to give Gizella whatever help she needed in the kitchen.

As good as it was to be with her parents, Vali knew she had

to return to Budapest as soon as possible. It wasn't a good idea to be away from her own home and its secrets for too long. So she said a somewhat uneasy goodbye to the three of them, and with a bulging basket of provisions, boarded the carriage back to the train station.

Soon afterwards a short article appeared in *Film Hiradó*, one of the entertainment magazines. It began: 'This year there hasn't been much news about summer holidays in the newspapers' theatre columns. We only know about a few such restful breaks. Vali Rácz, for example, has been relaxing with her parents in Gölle, in Somogy County . . .'

Five

The new date set by Eichmann for the commencement of deportations from Budapest, 5 August 1944, came and went. Once again, Horthy had cancelled it. And once again, an enraged Eichmann set a new one: 25 August. Such blatant and repeated opposition to his aims was unprecedented. Veesenmayer, too, demanded a resumption of the deportations, but in vain.

Now Horthy received support from a most unexpected source: Heinrich Himmler himself, SS Chief and Eichmann's superior, sent Horthy a telegram with his consent to the cessation of deportations.

Unlike the fanatical Eichmann, Himmler was a pragmatist. And he was beginning to see that the end of the Third Reich was not far off. Germany's military position was ever more precarious and on 20 July there had been an attempt by senior officers to assassinate Hitler. Confidence in the Führer was evaporating. So it was time for Himmler to start devising an alibi for himself, *vis-à-vis* the Allies. Written evidence of his agreement to end deportations might help him one day.

On 23 August, following a *coup d'état* in Rumania, that country surrendered to the Soviet forces and prepared to re-join the war on the side of the Allies. This encouraged Horthy who, resolved to consolidate his new, humanitarian position, a few days later dismissed Prime Minister Sztójay and replaced him with his loyal friend from the military, General Géza Lakatos.

A powerless Eichmann left Budapest in disgust, together

with his Special Operations Commando. He'd been recalled to Berlin, where he would soon be awarded the Iron Cross, 2nd Class, for his services in Hungary.

For the first time since the Occupation took place the previous March, the Jews of Budapest breathed more easily. It seemed as if Horthy might have won the tug-of-war over their destiny.

The same week which saw these crucial changes in the political situation of Hungary also brought a change to the daily life of Vali Rácz. It was on 20 August, St Stephen's Day (a Hungarian national holiday), that she received a visitor at the villa. Mihály Szüle was a playwright and the director of Budapest's Vidám Theatre. He had just written a new comedy, *Romeo and Piroska*, and had her in mind for one of the leading roles. Rehearsals were to begin in September and the play would open the season at the Vidám in early October. Was she interested?

He had just arrived that day from the country where his half-Jewish wife was living with forged Christian papers and working in the kitchen of a village inn. He arrived at Vali's house straight from the train station; he was weary, and she went into the kitchen to make him some coffee. Szüle was leaning against the kitchen door, talking to his hostess, when to his amazement he saw his good friend, Paul Barabás, emerging from the larder. And then he watched, speechless, as one after another the secret occupants followed Barabás up the stairs from the basement and through the larder door into the kitchen.

Szüle was one person whom they knew they could take into their confidence. An avowed anti-Nazi, he had steadfastly refused to kick out the Jewish actors and technicians employed by his theatre, even when that stance had become dangerous for him. And now, amused by the bewildered look on his face, Barabás and Vali explained who the Herzogs and the Mandels were and what they were doing there.

Szüle stayed for supper that night and they discussed his new play. Vali was delighted by the prospect of getting back to work again. Encouraged by Barabás, who said it would be good for her to get her mind off the burdens and anxieties of the

45

past several months, she accepted Süle's offer. She would be playing the role of a seductive, but mischievous actress in the play. It was tailor-made for her. That very evening they drew up a rough contract and signed their names to it.

Rehearsals began in the middle of September, according to schedule. And Vali threw herself eagerly into her work. But it wasn't long before a problem arose, a potentially lethal one.

Late one afternoon she arrived home from the theatre to receive a phone call from her father. He spoke in a tense and guarded voice from the office of the parish council, which had the only telephone in Gölle (of the old hand-cranked variety). He urged her to come at once.

She took the first train the next morning and spent the journey in agonizing speculation. She suspected that, whatever the problem, it had to do with Ilona, in which case the likely consequences could not be more grave.

She arrived to find her mother tearful and her father obviously very worried. They told her what had happened. It seemed that, after two months of hiding in their house and of not being able to go out, even for a short walk, Ilona had become extremely restless. She said she couldn't bear to be confined any longer, she had to get out, just for a little while. Ferenc and Gizella advised her against taking such a chance. But she was clearly upset and under stress, and so, in a careless moment, they relented, suggesting that Ilona accompany them to church the following Sunday morning.

Just the brief stroll over to the church and the pleasant intermingling with the Sunday gathering was enough to satisfy Ilona's longing for movement and a change of scene. Her spirits picked up. She sat through the mass beside Gizella, while Ferenc was at his usual place up in the choir, playing the organ. Unfamiliar as the young Jewess was with church music, she was as moved that morning by his beautiful singing of the hymns as any of the Catholics around her.

But the next day there was an unexpected caller at the Rácz house. It was the village notary, an important local functionary and a well-meaning man who had no desire to see the headmaster come to harm. He had come to warn him.

'There are rumours going around the village,' the notary began. 'You were seen at church yesterday in the company of an unknown woman, and now people are saying that she's been hiding here at your house. I don't know anything about this young woman, Mr Rácz, but if you are in any danger – please be careful. It won't be long before the rumours reach the ears of our gendarme.'

There was only one thing to be done, that was clear. Vali would have to take Ilona back to Budapest with her right away. Each moment longer that she remained in Gölle increased the chances of her being caught. She would simply have to join the others at the villa. Vali immediately called the railway station and booked two berths on the night train to Budapest. Once again, Vali Rácz would be travelling with her 'secretary'.

It was a subdued and regretful Ilona who parted from the Ráczes some hours later. She was pleased about one thing, though: she had put on a lot of weight. She'd spent most of her time in the kitchen – helping Gizella to bake bread and cakes and prepare rich, wholesome meals. (Her special task had been to churn the butter, which apparently also involved frequent tasting.) So she ate huge amounts, while getting hardly any exercise. She had been a slim girl before, and now, in her fattened-up condition, she looked quite different. It was a good disguise, making it more difficult for people to recognize her.

They arrived at the station late in the evening, shortly before the train was due. Security at all railway stations was very tight at that time, and especially for trains going to Budapest because most of those on the run – deserters, Jews, resisters of all kinds – would attempt to avoid detection amongst the crowds in the capital. They were greatly relieved to pass through the security checks. They were questioned, but no one suspected the identity of the plump secretary.

But when the train pulled in, they were alarmed to find it completely overrun by German soldiers. The berths in the sleeping cars had been requisitioned and all the carriages were overcrowded. Even the corridors were full of passengers who'd been evicted from their seats. Somehow or other a place was made available in one of the compartments for the *chanteuse*, but

47

her secretary could only sit on a case out in the cramped corridor. It was a long, uncomfortable and uneasy journey.

Neither Vali nor Ilona nor any of the other disgruntled passengers could have known then why there were so many soldiers on their night train. Yet the knowledge would undoubtedly have provoked strong, if mixed, feelings. For the Wehrmacht, on the verge of losing its Balkan Front, was retreating from Yugoslavia. Rumania and Bulgaria were already occupied by the Russians, and the Red Army was closing in. Allied landings on the Aegean coast were imminent. The Balkan Army led by General Weichs had been worn down by the ceaseless harassment from Yugoslav partisans and it was broken up into small units. Their only option now was to head north – to reinforce the Wehrmacht's position in Hungary.

★

Romeo and Piroska opened at the Vidám Theatre on 6 October. It was a success, providing the kind of escapist comedy entertainment which audiences crave during troubled times. The weekly magazine *Magyar Stage Play* carried a publicity photograph of Vali on its cover, in a suitably alluring pose.

But Vali had one problem which she did not anticipate. By this stage of the war it was becoming difficult to get around the city. Many vehicles had been requisitioned by the German and Hungarian armies, and there was also a shortage of petrol. There were few private cars on the streets and taxis were scarce. So getting back home at night after the performance was no easy matter. The Vidám Theatre was in the downtown business district of Pest, while the villa was across the river and up towards the Buda hills. The streetcars were still running, but late at night, worn out after the performance, Vali couldn't face being tossed around in one of those.

In this Vali was saved by another of the numerous men who were so smitten with her that they would do anything for her: József.

József was a doctor, first assistant to the famous Professor Ádám who had his surgery in one of the city clinics. He'd met Vali several months earlier when, having been recommended to her by a friend, he attended a minor injury to her leg. It wasn't long before his professional interest in her leg was overtaken by a personal interest in the rest of her. He was warm, solicitous, and a rather useful person to have around.

József was Jewish. But he was fortunate enough to have obtained excellent forged documents, which enabled him to continue practising as a 'Christian' doctor even after the Occupation. Then, in July, he found a new role for himself. For that was when a young Swedish diplomat, Raoul Wallenberg, arrived in Budapest and established 'Section C' of the Swedish Legation in Buda, concerned solely with rescuing Jews. One of the first things Wallenberg did was to accumulate a large staff of Hungarians, mainly Jews, to help him in his operations. He planned to set up two hospitals, and so he needed several doctors on his staff; József became one of them. As an ostensible Aryan he was able to get around the city easily and he was allocated the use of a Red Cross ambulance, one of several which the Swedish Legation managed to acquire.

And now that Vali was having trouble getting back from the theatre each night, it was in this ambulance that, whenever he could, he picked her up after the show and drove her home. Because of the black-out the city was very dark at night, and in any case those were dangerous days for a woman to be out late on her own. Sometimes, if József wasn't needed again until the next morning, he spent the night with her at the villa. He gave his calm and steady support not only to her, but to the five Jews hiding at the house.

It was a tight squeeze with five people in the hidden compartment of the wardrobe originally intended for only two. They tried it out to see how they would all fit in, in case the dreaded raid should, after all, take place. There wasn't an inch to spare. And things were made more uncomfortable by the fact that the wall on the left side slanted at a sharp angle as it ran parallel to the ceiling above the stairs, which meant that some of them couldn't even stand up straight, but had to lean awkward-ly against this wall. How long could someone hold such a position, motionless and in silence?

Early October was marked by another event: the arrival of

Vali's much-loved aunt, the gentle and soft-spoken Karolin, who had decided to evacuate her home to the northeast of Budapest in view of the advancing Russian Front. The Red Army was gradually forming a ring around Budapest – from the east they were battling their way to the north and south of the city. Only the west, where Hungary bordered on the Reich, remained for the time being under the control of the Wehrmacht.

News was spreading of the Russians' ruthless treatment of Hungary's civilian population, seen as allies of Hitler and historic enemies. Karolin, not unnaturally, had no desire to sit and wait it out. She was alone and vulnerable at the time because her husband Lajos was visiting his family in Gölle. So, their eleven-year-old daughter having been safely deposited at a residential convent school in Pest (run by the Order of the English Sisters, who also sheltered many Jewish children), she packed a few belongings and moved in with Vali. She left a message for Lajos at their flat, telling him where she'd gone and advising him to join her there.

Her life had not been easy since she married Lajos Esküdt and left Gölle. The Esküdt family was one of the oldest in the village, having been there, originally as serfs, since the eighteenth century. When the serfs were liberated in 1848, the Esküdts, along with the other families, were given a decent portion of land and became successful farmers.

Young Lajos rose to prominence during the 1920s under the government of Count Bethlen but his career had been tragically curtailed. He was an educated and enlightened man who remained, first and foremost, a representative of the peasant class from which he had originated. As a leading member of the Smallholders' Party and First Secretary to the then Minister of Agriculture, István Nagyatádi-Szabó, he campaigned to change Hungary's age-old, feudal land policies.

At that time, half the country's arable land was owned by some 2,000 landowners, a largely aristocracy/gentry stratum. There was a small class of wealthy peasants, and a vast population of poor, landless and ill-educated ones. Esküdt and Nagyatádi-Szabó attempted to bring in policies of reform

50

which would not only redistribute the land more justly, but create a broadly-based, educated 'middle class' within the peasantry. They realized that only by lifting the peasantry out of its lowly position in Hungarian society could they end the unjust divisions between the various strata.

But Bethlen, moderate and well-meaning though he was, remained to the end a faithful representative of *his* class – the landed aristocracy. Such radical reforms were anathema to him. Esküdt became an ever more outspoken critic of Bethlen's policies, until the Prime Minister resolved to silence him. While Nagyatádi-Szabó, ruined by failure, took his own life, the impassioned and volatile Esküdt spent several years interned in a mental asylum. It was common knowledge that he was interned not for mental but for political reasons, and the 'Esküdt affair' was a notorious issue at the time.

His hopes crushed, his career at an end, Esküdt was released, an embittered and resentful man. He was to spend the rest of his life struggling to be vindicated and compensated for his losses. Although he was a difficult man to live with, Karolin remained a devoted wife. Now, in addition to her personal cares, she had the invading Russians to worry about. No wonder she didn't want to be alone.

With Karolin the household, including Vali, had swollen to eight members, five of them clandestine. Every room was being used to the full. The Mandels were still in their basement bedroom, and Zsóka was using the one next to it because her own small front bedroom on the ground floor was being used by Margit and her daughter, Marietta. Ilona and Karolin slept on the first floor, in the bedroom next to Vali's.

Organizing enough food for so many people under wartime conditions was virtually a full-time occupation, so Zsóka was kept very busy. She had to be extremely discreet. As there were only three official occupants of the house, she constantly had to conceal the fact that she was buying for eight. She received a lot of help in the kitchen, though. Karolin was a superb cook, excelling in the subtleties of the Austro-Hungarian cuisine. She could also create wonders out of the odd selection of provisions that were available. Meat, for one thing, was becoming hard to obtain in sufficient quantities. Fortunately it was still possible to receive, once in a while, a parcel of food from Gölle.

Szerén, too, helped with the cooking. Of course, she had always been used to a kosher kitchen, but these were exceptional times. The Mandels ate whatever was available. They knew only too well that they had to suspend much of their traditional way of life, in order to stay alive. But they continued to observe the Friday night Sabbath in the basement, and Szerén still wore the customary wig.

★

It seemed during the early autumn weeks of 1944 as if the Jews of the Hungarian capital would, miraculously, be the lucky ones – the ones to survive the inferno of Hitler's Europe. In Regent Horthy they had a newly emboldened national leader, Prime Minister Lakatos was on their side, the Allies were beating back the Germans and they no longer suffered the evil presence of Eichmann. There were no more deportations. No trains to Auschwitz.

It was on 15 October, a peaceful Sunday, that Horthy made the final move in his political strategem – it was the culmination of his plans, both secret and public. At midday he made an announcement over Hungarian Radio: Hungary was withdrawing from the Axis camp and the war; it was suing for an armistice with the Allies.

There was great celebration at 47d Budakeszi Avenue. A cherished bottle of champagne was brought out and everyone drank a toast to the promised armistice and to the future. And indeed, shortly after the announcement, they saw the German tanks streaming up Budakeszi Avenue on their way out of the city.

Throughout Budapest the Jews of the yellow star houses, who had for months been cowering in fear for their lives, came out on to the streets and embraced each other. Weeping with relief, they ripped the stars off their clothes.

But later that day there was another announcement on the radio. This time it wasn't Horthy speaking, but someone of an altogether different complexion: Ferenc Szálasi, leader of the

Arrow Cross Party, Hungary's most vicious and rabidly anti-Semitic faction, modelled on the Nazis themselves. He informed the Hungarian people that the 'traitorous' Regent had been ousted, and that he was himself the new leader of the nation – both as prime minister and head of state.

He spoke the truth. Horthy, whose submission was assured by the kidnapping of his son, was already in German custody and shortly to be taken to the Reich. In a sudden strike to forestall the inadequately prepared armistice with the Allies and retain control over its wayward neighbour, Germany had launched its second military operation against Hungary. 'Operation Panzerfaust' sponsored the *coup d'état* which put the illegal Szálasi government into power.

Vali and the others watched in horror as the tanks, which had only a few hours earlier left the city, came rumbling back down Budakeszi Avenue again.

Forty-five years later Ilona, in recalling that sight, observed: 'All that had happened until then was as nothing. It was at that moment that our real terror began.'

Six

Adolf Eichmann, bloated with arrogant pride, returned to Budapest two days after the *coup d'état* to carry on where he left off in July. Rubbing his hands as he got off the plane, he told Hungarian government officials, 'You thought the events in Bulgaria and Rumania would be repeated here . . . but this government will work to *our* orders. The Jews will be deported on foot. We need our vehicles for other purposes.'

The brief respite enjoyed by the Jews of the capital was over. The new Interior Minister of the Arrow Cross government, Gábor Vajna, immediately issued a decree nullifying all foreign protective certificates. There were to be no more exemptions. Not even the decorated heroes of the First World War were safe any more. 'One-armed Imre' Herzog and others like him had to go into hiding.

Eichmann and Vajna planned to carry out their new programme by having 50,000 Jews march 120 miles to the notorious internment camp at Strasshof, near Vienna. The remainder were to be forced into a ghetto in District VII of central Pest, consisting of about 162 apartment houses, to be deported at a later stage. But first, both male and female Jews between the ages of sixteen and sixty were carried off *en masse* to dig trenches and work on fortification lines around Budapest. The Russian troops were not far now from its outer suburbs.

The headquarters of the Arrow Cross Party at 60 Andrássy Avenue, that great, grey building which they named the 'House of Loyalty', soon became the city's most infamous address.

Vali Rácz aged three, 1914

Vali with her parents — Gizella and Ferenc Rácz

A Sunday afternoon, the garden in Gölle

Graduation from the Kaposvár Girls' Gymnasium, 1931

In a favourite stage dress

In the first dress
designed for her by Sándor Gergely

Film still from *Toprini Nász* (Wedding in Toprin), 1939

At Paul Engel's castle in Dormánd, late 1930s

From *Toprini Nász* with co-star Ferenc Kiss

Franz Lehár
presents her with his song, 1940

In white tie and tails

Enjoying herself at Lake Balaton with Sándor Gergely and his sister, Janika.
Vali is on the bicycle that was stolen during the Siege

Black taffeta dress for the Villon ballads

At home in Budakeszi Avenue. On the right is the cabinet
behind which Marietta would hide

47d Budakeszi Avenue,
Vali's home from 1939 to 1956

Concert at the Kroll Opera, Berlin, 1943

During the Berlin visit,
outside Hotel Adlon with the singer
Sári Barabás (no relation to Paul)

Countless victims were to be dragged there and tortured in its underground cells.

As soon as they assumed power, the Arrow Cross demanded that former Prime Minister Miklós Kállay be handed over to them. Kállay had sought refuge in the Turkish Embassy at the time of the March 19th invasion and it had been his sanctuary ever since. The Arrow Cross now threatened to burn the building down unless Kállay came out. He agreed to leave the embassy. The Arrow Cross wanted to execute him at once, but the Germans, who still had the upper hand, chose to deport him to Mauthausen concentration camp.

Miss Arizona, owner of the famous nightclub frequented in the 1930s by the Prince of Wales, now met her tragic end. The Arrow Cross closed down the nightclub and took her Jewish husband away. (Her son had already committed suicide when called in for labour service.) Anxious to save her husband, she made a deal with the SS – he would be returned unharmed in exchange for a large sum of money and her considerable collection of jewellery. She was picked up one day by a couple of SS officers, together with her fortune, and driven away. She believed she was being taken to her husband. But her husband had already been deported or killed. He was never seen again. And the life of the sensational and exotic Miss Arizona came to an abrupt end when the Germans stopped their car somewhere along the Danube, shot her and threw her body into the water.

The comedy *Romeo and Piroska* continued to play to amused and appreciative audiences night after night at the Vidám, as if the world outside the theatre were the make-believe one. By night Vali played her part as the trouble-making but ultimately good-hearted actress, by day she concerned herself with the complex affairs at 47d Budakeszi Avenue.

One night after the performance the stage manager went to see Vali in her dressing room with a singular request. The audience generally contained its share of German soldiers, and on that particular evening two middle-ranking officers of the Wehrmacht had approached him with a view to securing an introduction to her. 'It seems,' the stage manager explained warily, 'that they wish to invite you out for dinner.'

Vali had been changing into her street clothes, in preparation for going home. Now she stopped abruptly and stared at him. But before she could reply, he appealed to her in a hushed, urgent voice.

'Please . . . it would be advisable to accept their invitation. They seem polite enough. Just a dinner – no strings attached. If you refuse it could be unpleasant, for all of us.'

It only took a moment's thought for Vali to realize that the stage manager was right. It was not only better from the theatre's point of view, the dinner with the officers would also help to avert any suspicions about her. A definite advantage when she was hiding five Jews in her home.

The two officers were indeed courteous, as well as admiring. They were attractive men in their late thirties, and delighted that their invitation had been accepted. They drove her to one of the city's best restaurants, the Duna Room of the Gellért Hotel, and there, over an excellent meal and a couple of bottles of the best Hungarian wine, they chatted amiably about the theatre, films and Vali's career. The officers were entranced by their dinner companion, a condition helped along by the romantic strains of the resident gypsy orchestra. Vali, in good form, regaled them with carefully chosen anecdotes about her visit to Germany a year and a half earlier.

In the spring of 1943 she had been asked to take part in a mammoth 'Magyar Evening' to be staged at the ornate Kroll State Opera House in Berlin. (It was there that the Reichstag had been holding its sessions ever since the burning of the Reichstag building in 1933.) The two Hungarian radio orchestras, together with an array of singers and dancers, were to travel by overnight train to Berlin. The charity concert was organized by Döme Sztójay, then Hungarian Ambassador to Berlin, to aid the German victims of the previous winter's military catastrophe on the Eastern Front.

Vali had been reluctant to venture into the heart of the Reich, a city suffering from frequent bombing raids. And in any case, she was busy appearing each night at the Hangli Kioszk. But the Rónay brothers persuaded her to go. They told her that if she refused, they would themselves get into trouble. The authorities would claim that, as Jews, the Rónays had forbidden her to perform in Berlin.

So Vali joined the troupe. She was pleased in a way, after all. As the war had made foreign travel very difficult, she had not been abroad for a long time. It felt good to be going on a long trip again. And she would be able to get together with Paul Barabás, who was then in Berlin directing *Frau am Steuer* (Woman at the Steering Wheel) at the UFA Studios. The film, which he wrote himself, starred the famous Austrian actress, Lilian Harway.

At dawn, as the train went through the outskirts of Berlin, Vali was to get her first taste of the large-scale devastation of war. Bombed houses, the burnt-out wreckages of vehicles, great heaps of rubble – these were the sights which lined the railway tracks. The experience was both depressing and alarming.

But life in Berlin went on with a remarkable normality. The company took a sight-seeing tour in a glass-topped bus and saw that the shops and cafés were busy; the great metropolis was full of life, despite the constant reminders of death: the results of the bombing raids.

They stayed at the Hotel Adlon, where in previous years the top Nazis, the men closest to Hitler, held their *bierabends* – beer evenings. At these informal gatherings, over beer and sausages, they expounded their beliefs and justified their doings to invited foreign correspondents and diplomats. The *bierabends* were hosted by Alfred Rosenberg, the Nazi Party's ludicrous in-house 'philosopher'.

The 'Magyar Evening', presented to an audience rife with German soldiers on leave, the SS and members of the Nazi leadership, was a resounding success. Vali sang several Magyar folk songs dressed in a bright, exquisitely embroidered folk costume.

After the concert there was a reception at the Hungarian Embassy, where Vali chatted with a highly gratified Sztójay, and mingled with the Nazi top brass. The next day Barabás introduced her to some producers from UFA. They were interested in her, having seen her performance. Barabás urged her to come to Berlin for a while. She would be in demand, be offered good film parts and have great success. Perhaps, too, he simply wanted to have her near him.

Vali declined. While understandably attracted to the idea of becoming internationally as well as nationally known, the war made everything seem uncertain, and risky. She had her first experience of bombing at close hand during the company's three days in Berlin. It was enough to put her off the notion of living there.

On the day of her return, Barabás took her on a hasty shopping expedition. Vali spent the modest fee she had earned from the concert on stage make-up, cosmetics, perfumes and toiletries. She stocked up because, air raids or no air raids, there was still a greater variety of those commodities in Berlin than in Budapest . . .

And so the dinner at the Gellért with the two Wehrmacht officers went very well and ended with gallant hand kissing at the front gate of Vali's house. Feeling it seemly for her to reciprocate in some way, she invited them for drinks the following week, early one evening before she left for the theatre. They agreed upon a date.

There was an ulterior motive, too, for her invitation. She deliberately wanted the German army jeep to be seen parked in front of the house, to give the neighbourhood the impression that she was on affable terms with the Germans and couldn't possibly be harbouring Jews. If only she had known then that this move, so shrewd and expedient in those days, would, when times had changed, put her in mortal danger.

Vali warned the five fugitives to keep absolutely quiet in the basement on the evening of the officers' visit. The one thing she dreaded was an air raid, in which case *everyone* would have to take shelter in the basement. By then, Allied air attacks had become commonplace in Budapest, too.

Luckily, there was no air raid that evening. The officers came, bringing Vali a bunch of flowers, and after their drinks and an admiring look around the elegant ground floor, they drove her across the river to the theatre. There she received more hand kisses in parting.

58

She never saw either of them again.

★

In the first week of November, the death marches began. There were no more cattle trains available and the only way to deport the Jews of Budapest was on foot. Men and women were rounded up and herded westwards to the border at Hegyeshalom, there to be handed over to the Germans as fodder for slave labour. They were treated with such bestiality by their armed escort that even a member of the Waffen-SS – General Hans Jüttner – lodged a formal complaint with the SS authorities. The majority perished along the way and when the half-dead remainder finally reached the border the Germans considered them unfit for anything but the extermination camps. Very few who took part in a forced march to Hegyeshalom ever returned.

As long ago as December 1941, Hitler had issued his so-called *Nacht und Nebel Erlass* – Night and Fog Decree. According to this decree, anyone endangering German security, any 'enemies of the Reich', were to vanish without a trace, literally into the night and fog. Innumerable people did disappear in this way following the fateful knock on the door in the middle of the night. It prevented the rest of the population from seeing what was going on and becoming restive and troublesome.

The decree was applied to the Jews of Budapest, too, during those barbarous November weeks. Vali witnessed this herself late one night on the way home from dining with friends after the theatre. She had ordered a taxi and the driver took her along the Károly Körút, a main thoroughfare in Pest, running parallel to the Danube. The taxi suddenly slowed down. Vali peered through the window and saw a moving mass of people, the individual figures barely discernible in the darkness of the blacked-out city. There were about two hundred of them walking silently in a column, five or six abreast, heading north from the inner city. They were all carrying something – a small suitcase or a bundle.

'Who are those people?' Vali asked the driver. 'Where are they walking to?'

'I'm not sure,' he replied. 'I think they might be Jews . . .'

59

'Stop for a moment.'

The taxi pulled up alongside the kerb and Vali rolled down the window. The dark, hunched figures walked past the taxi, only a few feet away, and Vali could now see their faces. They were the most dejected collection of people imaginable. Alarmed by the sight, she called out to them. What was happening? Where were they going?

But no one dared stop even for an instant; no one dared speak to her. Then Vali caught sight of the armed guards escorting the column.

The taxi driver did, too. He turned to Vali and spoke in an edgy voice. 'We must go on. Please . . . it's dangerous.'

A moment later the taxi swung out into the road again and soon left the marching people behind. Vali continued to look back, hardly able to tear her eyes away, almost bursting with pity. The dark figures merged once more into the night.

'Do you know where they are being taken?' asked Vali.

'I've heard it rumoured that they're put into the brickyard at Óbuda, before being moved on.'

The next day Vali described what she had seen to the Mandels and Margit Herzog. They talked about it for a long while, wondering what it could all mean. Were they being resettled in the countryside? Put to work in factories in Germany? None of them could yet imagine that those silent, cowed figures were simply marching to their deaths. It was a sight that would remain with Vali forever.

She learned more about the Jews' lamentable predicament from József, who still frequently drove her home at night from the theatre. Sometimes he stopped along the way at one of Wallenberg's 'safe-houses' to tend to the ill.

It was after the October 15th *coup* that Wallenberg's Jew-saving work really began in earnest. When the Arrow Cross assumed power, Sweden immediately broke off diplomatic relations with the new government, making it virtually impossible for the Swedish Legation to operate in Budapest. Yet the staff of the Legation, strongly influenced by Wallenberg, voted to stay on rather than pack up and return to Sweden. He saw only too clearly that the Jews needed him now more than

60

ever, and he was about to prove that, even in the face of an unspeakably heinous enemy, the innocent could be saved by nothing more than courage and imagination.

Wallenberg increased his staff to four hundred. József was now one of forty doctors working for him. He also acquired many more 'protected' buildings, bearing the Swedish flag. These quickly became packed with the families he had so far managed to rescue with his protective passports. By appealing for support to the young wife of Arrow Cross Foreign Minister Gábor Kemény, a woman who sympathized with Wallenberg, he managed to get the order nullifying all foreign protective documents revoked. But although his safe-houses were officially off-bounds to the roving gangs of Arrow Cross thugs, that didn't mean they weren't frequently attacked by them. So Wallenberg bribed the Arrow Cross. He gave them food from the Swedish stocks in exchange for protection for his buildings. This often worked.

When he learned about the death marches to Hegyeshalom, he mounted rescue operations of incredible verve and initiative. He set up checkpoints along the route and managed to remove some of the marchers on the basis of their protective documents. He also dispensed food and medical aid to as many people as he could, giving a new will to survive to some of those about to give up. On one occasion he went to Hegyeshalom, clutching a stack of Swedish passports, as the marchers arrived. He told the Arrow Cross guards who he was and ordered them to stand aside as he searched for Jews entitled to the passports. The guards responded by surrounding him with pointed bayonets. But Wallenberg shouted above their heads that he had Swedish passes for anyone who had lost their documents. Throughout the wretched, despairing group of deportees, hands were raised high in the air. With a masterful conviction, he persuaded the officer in charge that he should be allowed to remove all those who had raised their hands. He distributed his documents to them and promptly led his protégés away.

Wallenberg saved lives in other ways, too. Later, in early December, when the water supply of Budapest was damaged by Allied air attacks, he had his team of doctors inoculate everyone in his overcrowded buildings against typhoid and cholera. This prevented the epidemics which would doubtless have killed thousands.

★

The illegally established Arrow Cross government of Ferenc Szálasi was unable to enlist the support of most of the Hungarian army. The commanders of the First and Second Armies, Generals Miklós and Vörös, refused to follow Arrow Cross orders. Many of their troops laid down their arms and went home. Around Budapest, however, under the control of the Wehrmacht, Hungarian troops were still being whipped into action against the advancing Russians.

Colonel-General Friessner, commanding the Wehrmacht's *Heeresgruppe Sud* in Hungary, was well aware of the unreliability of the Hungarian military. It was one of the reasons for his recommendation to German High Command that Budapest be made into an 'open city' as, for example, in the case of Rome. This would allow the Germans to retreat and cut their losses, leaving the Russians simply to walk in and occupy it. Friessner did not believe that the Wehrmacht could hold the city.

But Hitler totally rejected this recommendation. His unequivocal order was that Budapest must be defended to the very end – he wanted the Red Army detained in the Hungarian capital as long as possible, in order to win time for the defence of the next city in line for attack: Vienna. Budapest would have to be turned into a 'fortress', and if it came to it, the city would have to be defended street by street, and house by house. Budapest became the sacrifice in the cause of the Reich's defence.

Desertions from the Hungarian army were rife. Captured deserters were dealt with mercilessly and instantly. As a deterrent to others, they were simply hanged from the nearest tree or lamp-post. The swinging corpses of soldiers became a common sight on the streets of Budapest during the final months of 1944.

It was in the second week of November that, with the house

nearly filled to bursting point, one last fugitive came to join the others at Vali Rácz's house. Not a Jew, but a nineteen-year-old deserter. Zsóka's son.

When the housekeeper appealed to her for refuge for her son, Vali felt that she had no choice but to take the young man in. By this time she was no longer so certain of Zsóka's loyalty. As the number of Jews in the house had increased, and the risks had increased correspondingly, Zsóka had grown visibly discontented with the situation. It began to cross Vali's mind that Zsóka might one day decide she had had enough and denounce her. So taking her son in was a kind of insurance policy.

Zsóka's son was not an unpleasant young man. He was thin, of medium height and dark-haired like his mother. But unlike Zsóka, he was rather intelligent. He was reserved and spent most of his time in the kitchen with his mother. At night he slept on the kitchen floor.

It wasn't long before Vali and the others realized that Zsóka was secretly pilfering from their precious food supplies in order to give her son more than his fair share. She baked cakes for him, using up inordinate amounts of one of the scarcest commodities – sugar. Vali, still dependent on Zsóka's co-operation, said nothing. But she resolved to get rid of the housekeeper when those desperate times were over.

It was now impossible for all the fugitives to fit into the secret compartment behind the wardrobe. It wasn't just the lack of space but that the weight of so many people was putting undue strain on the staircase ceiling. In order to ease the strain, Marietta was given another hiding place.

On the right side of the sitting room there were two perpendicular walls lined with tall, antique bookcases and elaborate bench-style seats. This was the dining area. In the corner, where the two walls met, there was a large, carved cabinet, which appeared to be an integral part of the whole fixed unit. But in fact the cabinet was free-standing, and could be pulled out from its position. Although unsuitable for the average adult, there was just enough standing room behind it for a slim young girl.

Marietta, at only fourteen, was courageous and self-assured.

It was very hard for this lively teenager to spend months of her life shut up in a house, unable to go outside or take part in any normal activities, and isolated from others of her age. But Marietta possessed an understanding beyond her years. When she felt the strain of her confinement too intensely, she went to one of the rear windows of the house and sat for a long time, gazing out at the world and breathing the fresh air from the garden. It was in this way that, during those cold November weeks, she developed a bad cough.

As the disintegration of the armed forces continued apace, the Szálasi government announced ever more stringent measures against deserters. On 25 November, Interior Minister Gábor Vajna issued his most merciless decree yet: the death sentence applying to army deserters was to be extended to members of the deserters' families.

But Vali didn't have much time to worry about this. Because on the morning of the following day, Sunday, 26 November, the unthinkable happened. Agents of Péter Hain's dreaded Secret Police raided 47d Budakeszi Avenue. And Vali Rácz became a 'guest' at the notorious Hotel Majestic.

Seven

That Saturday night after the performance, József had driven her home in the Red Cross ambulance as he so often did. He had finished his work for the night, so Vali asked him to stay until morning. Exhausted after working his usual eighteen-hour day, he gratefully accepted the offer. It was around midnight when they both finally fell asleep.

At ten o'clock in the morning they were still sleeping heavily when, all of a sudden, they were woken up by people rushing frantically into the bedroom, clambering over the bed and bolting into the wardrobe.

'Gestapo!' someone cried. 'They're at the gate!'

József clasped Vali's hand. 'Stay calm. We know exactly what to say.'

They could hear Zsóka downstairs, calling across the garden from the front door – 'Just a moment! I'm looking for the key to the gate!' She was delaying as long as possible, to give everyone time to hide, but she dared not delay too long. It took a while for the heavy cabinet to be pulled away from the wall so that Marietta could squeeze in behind it.

Soon Zsóka was leading two plainclothes policemen down the path towards the house. By now József was dressed. Vali had put on a dressing gown. They embraced, and went downstairs together.

They found Zsóka, confronted by the two men in the hallway, insisting emphatically that she was not Margit Herzog but merely the housekeeper. Apparently, Zsóka answered the description they'd been given of a short, dark-haired woman in her early forties. But it soon became obvious enough that Zsóka was indeed a simple housekeeper and not the cosmopolitan daughter of a wealthy landowner.

They turned to Vali. 'Valéria Rácz? We have orders to search this house.'

Vali felt her throat going completely dry, as always when she was frightened. 'Search . . . for what?'

'Whom have you been hiding here?' one of the men demanded loudly.

'No one'.

József spoke now, with quiet self-assurance. 'It's all right, Vali. Let them search the house. They'll soon see there is no one hiding here.'

'And who are you?' they challenged him.

József told them his name and showed them his identity documents. 'I am a close friend of Miss Racz's. I brought her home last night from the theatre. It was late, so I spent the night here.' The men scrutinized his papers. They were all in order. Grudgingly, they handed the papers back.

'I can verify,' József began, 'that Miss Rácz has done nothing . . .'

But the men just waved him aside and began their search. One of them went upstairs, and the other, with a bloodhound's instinct, demanded to know whether the house had a basement. Zsóka led the way into the kitchen and pointed out the stairs leading down from the larder.

Vali stood out in the hallway. Her throat was so parched by now that she was barely able to swallow. There were two slept-in beds in the basement. Added to the others upstairs, it was immediately obvious that more beds had been slept in than by the number of people allegedly sleeping at the house. Vali knew the explanation she would give. That had all been worked out before, with Paul Barabás. But would they believe her? She wished that Karolin was at home: she needed her support. But her aunt had gone to mass at a nearby church.

The policeman came thundering up the stairs from the basement. 'The sheets on those beds down there,' he said

66

menacingly, 'are still warm. Who slept in them last night?'

Vali tried to speak matter-of-factly. 'My relatives have been visiting from Somogy County. They left only a little while ago.'

He stared at her incredulously. Then, a moment later, he pushed past her and went upstairs to join his partner.

As soon as the two men entered Vali's bedroom they opened the wardrobe door, rifled through the clothes and ran their hands along the back and side walls. Behind the thin partition, the Mandels, Margit, Ilona and the young deserter stood crammed together, some of them holding desperately on to the sloping side wall, praying that they wouldn't slip, that there would be no involuntary movement, no creaking shoe to give them away.

After the wardrobe, they searched every inch of the bedroom for the incriminating evidence they were convinced must be there. They emptied drawers and looked through letters. It all took time. Meanwhile the hidden people waited in agonizing stillness and the secret compartment became ever more airless and stifling. Eventually, the men left the bedroom and went back down to the sitting room.

They sat down at the dining table before the bookcases and the cabinet behind which Marietta stood, barely breathing. She listened nervously to the conversation of the two policemen. With each minute she became more terrified because she had a growing urge to cough. Would she be able to stop herself? They were sitting no more than four or five feet away from her and the smallest noise would give her away.

The men were studying the papers in a file, leafing through them, one by one, discussing the details of their morning's work. Then Marietta heard them mention two names – her mother's and her own. They mentioned the Herzog family mansion at 106 Andrássy Avenue, as well as the address of the flat in Buda where Margit, her husband and children had been living. Marietta grew faint.

At last the men put their file away. They summoned Vali and ordered her to get dressed as she would have to go back to their headquarters with them.

Upstairs, as she opened the wardrobe to get some clothes to

67

wear, Vali whispered a few words to the five hidden behind the wall, to let them know what was happening. She put on a warm knitted dress and a pair of fur-lined half-boots. She took nothing with her but a handbag as she felt sure she would be released the same day. After all, the policemen had found no one hiding in the house. She put on a coat and scarf, then walked downstairs slowly and calmly, putting on her gloves.

The men had arrived on foot, and now they instructed József to drive them back to their headquarters on Swabian Hill. When they opened the front door of the house, Vali stepped out into a dense fog. It was almost impossible to see as far as the road. She was led up the path, put into the back of the Red Cross ambulance, and driven away unseen into the murky, ominous morning. Another implementation of the Night and Fog Decree.

As soon as they had gone, Zsóka hauled the cabinet away from the wall and Marietta staggered out. She was in a state of panic.

'I won't stay here and die!' she cried. 'I've got to get away!'

Zsóka tried to calm her down.

'Please,' Marietta beseeched her, 'give me a few pengős – I've got to leave this house *now*.'

Zsóka gave her some money. Marietta grabbed her coat from the small bedroom where she and her mother had been sleeping for the past five months and Zsóka let her out of the front gate. The young girl hurried down Budakeszi Avenue towards the city.

Then Zsóka went upstairs to let the others know it was safe to leave the wardrobe. Margit was horrified to learn that her daughter had disappeared. Where would she go? And how long could she last on her own, with nothing but a few pengős in her pocket? Somehow Margit would have to find her.

The five fugitives planned their escape from the house, which they all knew was now imperative. They left a few hours later. One by one, as inconspicuously as possible, they slipped out through the gate and into the fog. Each was heading for some specific destination, to a friend or contact who perhaps, with luck, would be able to give them shelter for a while . . . if they didn't get arrested by the police or abducted by Arrow Cross thugs along the way.

*

The five-storey Hotel Majestic nestled in the bend of a narrow side road at the top of Swabian Hill, surrounded by tall trees. Its rear windows and balconies commanded a terrific view of the city. By the time Vali Rácz arrived there, the building was already well-known to local residents as a place of torture; the anguished screams in the middle of the night attested to that.

An apprehensive József left Vali and the two policemen at the entrance. Driving his ambulance back down the hill towards the city, he knew he had to find Paul Barabás at once and let him know what had happened. Through his association with Wallenberg, József knew only too well about the workings of the Gestapo. They would not necessarily release a prisoner for lack of evidence of guilt. Vali could be in greater danger than she realized.

She was taken to a room on the second floor which had a guard posted at its door. It was already crammed with some forty-odd prisoners – men and women, the elderly and even children. It was stifling and pervaded by a palpable sense of fear and despair. Almost everyone was on the floor because there was no furniture in the room besides one short wooden bench. When Vali entered, everyone immediately recognized her and she was given a place to sit on the bench.

Although the room was crowded, it was quiet. People didn't talk much to one another. They were too frightened. They didn't know whom to trust. There could be informers amongst them. So they sat in silence, awaiting their fate.

Vali worried about Karolin. She would have come home by now from church to find that the police had taken her away. Vali could imagine her aunt's anguish. They were very close. At least her parents, safe in Gölle, were unaware of her predicament.

She also thought about the play, *Romeo and Piroska*. There was a matinée that afternoon. What would they all think when she didn't turn up? There was no understudy; they would have

69

to cancel the performance. She wasn't even allowed to call Mihály Szüle to let him know she was being detained.

But Szüle already knew. He, too, had received a call that morning from agents of the secret police. They went to see him at his office at the Vidám Theatre. They were polite and friendly, trying to win his confidence. Szüle poured them drinks. They told him that Vali had been taken into custody and would not be able to perform that day. What did he know about her? Who were her friends? What were her political leanings?

Szüle, also polite and friendly, said he had never discussed politics with her and knew nothing of her leanings. His association with her, he assured them, was purely professional. He didn't know about her private life. He said nothing about his visit to her house the previous summer, and he never mentioned Barabás's name.

After the policemen left, he set about cancelling that afternoon's performance. And he wondered what to tell the press when they made their inevitable inquiries.

Later that day at the Majestic a guard led Vali down to an interrogating room on the ground floor. There, to her amazement, she was interrogated by a young man she recognized at once from her school days in Kaposvár. He'd been a pupil at the boys' gymnasium there, across the street from the girls' gymnasium attended by Vali. They used to pass each other frequently on their way to and from school. Now he was Hain's right-hand man. He remembered Vali, too. But he didn't acknowledge it. The expression on his face was forbidding.

All of his questions were about Margit Herzog; he didn't seem to know anything about the others who had been hiding at the house. It was obvious that however her denunciation came about, it had to be connected with the Herzogs.

'Naturally, I admit that I know Margit,' Vali told the dour policeman from Kaposvár. 'And she did come to visit me at Budakeszi Avenue, once or twice. But she never stayed there.'

'We have information to the contrary.'

'Then your information is wrong.'

His manner became threatening. 'We will just have to keep you here until you co-operate.' He ordered the guard who had

70

been waiting by the door to take her back upstairs.

Vali began to realize that she would not be allowed home that day. She wished she had brought something with her – a toothbrush, some soap. That night she was given the privilege of sleeping on the hard bench, rather than the floor. The guard at the door, a tall, good-looking peasant boy who was not as cruel as he could have been, took pity on the *chanteuse*. He gave her his pair of thick, fur-lined leather gloves to use as a pillow, and he brought her a cup of weak coffee.

She woke up suddenly in the middle of the night to the sound of the door being violently flung open. She sat up and watched in horror as a young woman was dragged into the room by her hair, then thrown on to the floor like a sack of rubbish. She'd been badly beaten and was only half-alive. She was lifted up and carried to a corner by her family; her parents, husband and five-year-old son were all there.

The next day Vali befriended this tragic family. Like everyone else in the room (except Vali herself), they were Jewish. These prisoners, though, were all suspected of having committed other crimes besides the underlying crime of being Jewish. They had withheld information of importance to the authorities, or hidden their valuables. In any case, there was something to be tortured out of them. Had they been of no use, they would already have been deported or put into the ghetto.

Vali was forbidden to telephone anyone. But she trusted that by now József had reached Barabás. He would know what to do. He would get her out of this nightmare somehow. She prayed that she would not have to wait too long.

Meanwhile one grim, frightening day followed another, and her anxiety grew. Still there was no sign of her release. She slept very badly and not only because she lay on a wooden bench in an airless, crowded room: sometimes she was woken in the night by terrible cries and screams. These sounds of human suffering which reverberated through the corridors of the Majestic were unbearable to her.

She suddenly recalled that spring morning in 1942 when she was walking up Budakeszi Avenue and came across an old Swabian peasant driving a nanny goat and her two kids down

71

the street. He was whipping them with a stick to make them go faster, and the little black-and-white kids were protesting in weak, fearful voices. Vali couldn't stand it. She bought the kids then and there and took them home. She gave them the run of the garden. The press loved the story: she was photographed holding the two little goats on her lap like children. It was only some weeks later, when they had devoured all the expensive plants and flowers she'd planted, that she regretfully gave them away to a farm.

But what could she do now for the people in this ghastly abyss? She was as helpless as the rest of them.

She was interrogated again by Hain's assistant from Kaposvár, who was angry and frustrated by his lack of progress.

On Wednesday, 29 November, the following paragraph appeared in the *National News*, a daily paper: 'Following a few days of illness, Vali Rácz is once again appearing in the Vidám Theatre's *Romeo and Piroska*. The popular performer has had great success each evening with her satirical interpretation of an actress.'

Once again, the papers got it wrong. Szüle had informed the press that Vali was ill, and the play closed for two days while he hastily found a substitute and rehearsed her in the role. He had no idea when Vali would return, but the show had to continue. When it reopened on Tuesday, it was with the substitute, not Vali.

After the failure of the man from Kaposvár to get anywhere with Vali, Péter Hain decided on a new approach. Not torture. Even he, immoral and brutal as he was, stopped short of torturing such a popular and Aryan national figure as Vali Rácz. After all, people would take notice of such a thing, there would be disapproval. No, he would have to try something different.

When she was next brought down to the interrogation room, she found herself facing a young man with a broad smile who declared that he was her greatest fan. He offered her coffee, and seemed totally uninterested in the subject of the Herzogs. All he wanted to talk about was music. He confessed, somewhat shyly, that his ambition was to become an operatic tenor. He wanted to know all about the life of a professional singer.

He was either a rotten interrogator or he was following a particularly oblique method of extracting information.

Vali and the would-be tenor spent an hour or so chatting about vocal techniques, concerts and recordings. Then the guard took a nonplussed Vali back upstairs.

Later that day she received a small consolation. Her anxious Aunt Karolin, who'd been told by József where Vali was, had brought a parcel to the Majestic for her. It contained a towel, a blanket and a few toiletries. There was a bathroom adjoining the chamber where the prisoners were kept. (The Majestic had been built as a hotel, not a prison.) Now at least she could brush her teeth there and wash her face.

The following morning, as she was being led downstairs yet again to the interrogation room, she saw a woman and a small boy standing before the window on the first-floor landing, as though waiting for Vali and her guard to pass. The woman watched Vali intently as she descended the stairs towards them. She held the boy, who was about four or five, by the hand. He stood silently and without expression, paying little attention to Vali. And Vali only gave them a brief glance, before turning the corner and continuing down the next flight of stairs. She wondered vaguely for a moment who the poor child was and what he could be doing there.

(She found out some time after the war that the little boy was Péter, Margit Herzog's son. Captured by Hain's men, he'd been brought to the Majestic specifically for this stage-managed scene. The woman with him was a police guard. The idea was to bring him face to face with Vali, and evince a spontaneous reaction from the child. He would cry out in recognition and inquire after his mother, whom he would naturally know to be staying at Vali's house. But because Margit had shrewdly sent Péter out for a walk with the nanny on the day that Vali had called on her, the two of them had never seen each other before. After the failure of this ruse, the boy was dumped without further ado into the Budapest ghetto.)

Soon after her talks with the 'tenor' began, there was a new arrival in the densely packed room – an attractive young blonde woman, who immediately secured a place for herself on the

73

bench next to Vali and struck up a conversation.

'We have to stick together,' the blonde whispered to her, 'we're the only Christians here.' She encouraged Vali to talk about herself, and about why she was being interned.

But Vali had no intention of confiding in her. She had never before been a prisoner of the secret police, but she saw clearly enough that this 'friendly' Christian bore all the hallmarks of a not-too-clever informer.

Late one afternoon the blonde woman told Vali that she'd been given the task of taking a basketful of washing down to the laundry room in the annexe, across the road. It was heavy. Would Vali help her carry it?

The thought of spending a moment outside was so tempting that she couldn't refuse. They lifted the basket up from either side and carried it down the staircase. No guard accompanied them.

Vali paused outside the annexe on the way back from the laundry room. After the sickening, fetid air upstairs it was blissful to be out in the fresh, cool breeze of the verdant hillside. And after so many days of being crammed together with forty others, to be *almost* alone.

It was then that the thought struck her. She wasn't being guarded. Why not? She was out in the open, only a few feet from the road, with no one but her blonde companion, who seemed to be studiously looking in another direction. As if daring her, *willing* her to make a run for it. It was too quiet. Someone, somewhere, had to be watching. Vali became alarmed. What if this was a trap? They might be tempting her to try to escape, so that they could shoot her down. That would be justifiable murder, wouldn't it? Prisoners were never allowed to escape. Everyone knew that.

She picked up the laundry basket and called out to her companion, 'We'd better go back, hadn't we?' And they returned in uneasy silence to the oppressive room on the second floor.

At the end of November Vera Somló arrived with her mother. Vera was a slender, twenty-four-year-old Jewess with red hair and striking features. Since the Arrow Cross *coup*, she

74

had been posing as a Christian schoolteacher from Kiskunhalas, a refugee from the Russian advance. She'd also been working for a Hungarian resistance organization, distributing leaflets and firearms. One of their number turned out to be an informer, and they were betrayed to the SS.

Before she was brought to the Majestic, Vera had already been tortured for many days at the Markó Street Prison to make her reveal the names of the others in the organization. Its leader had managed to escape during the SS raid; now her torturers demanded to know who and where he was. Vera's forearms were raw where, day after day, cigarettes had been extinguished on them. But her spirit and determination to survive had not been crushed.

Vali was drawn to the courageous young woman and they soon became friends, to the annoyance of the blonde on the bench. Vera told Vali about herself. The daughter of the director of the well-known Dante Publishing Company, her background was liberal and intellectual. She was fluent in four languages and had planned to follow her father into the publishing world as an editor specializing in translations of French classics. Her Ph.D. thesis had been on Anatole France.

But the German occupation intervened. She and her mother were forced into a yellow star house. Only her father, a decorated hero of the First World War, was still able to carry on a more or less normal life . . . until 15 October. Then, through Vera's younger sister, who had forged links with Wallenberg, the family obtained false documents. Vera's father moved into a villa on Rose Hill, posing as a retired colonel. Vera and her mother chose to fight the Nazis through the resistance.

There was not much Vali could say to comfort her new friend, in constant pain from the open wounds on her arms, or the others in the room. But one night she did the only thing she could think of to calm and reassure her fellow prisoners: she sang to them. And she sang to them in English. At that time and especially in that place, to sing an English song was an act of deliberate defiance, tantamount to a political statement.

The song she chose was *My Bonnie Lies Over the Ocean*. The symbolic 'bonnie', as all who heard her understood, was

America – the saviour-nation desperately longed for by everyone staring into the jaws of the Nazi death-machine. (Only the small band of underground hardline Communists hoped the Russians would get there first.)

'. . . bring back, bring back, oh bring back my bonnie to me, to me . . .'

Her voice entered the darkness and despair, soothing, giving hope. Some were lulled to sleep by it.

But the tortured victims at the Majestic were not the only ones to be frightened. Their captors, too, were increasingly apprehensive. The Arrow Cross government had already begun its flight westward to Sopron, near the Austrian border. The Gestapo knew exactly how near the Red Army was by then. The city was almost completely surrounded. They could see that time was running out for them. And so, like savage animals when they are trapped, they became more dangerous than ever.

★

Paul Barabás had been racking his brains for a way to get Vali out ever since József got in touch with him on the day of her arrest. That first evening the two men discussed the dire predicament at length. Paul and József were very different types. They came from disparate backgrounds, barely knew each other and, what was more, were rivals for Vali's affection. But they instantly became close allies in striving for her release. Together they pondered the possibilities.

Clearly, Barabás had a better chance of helping Vali than József, a Jew operating with false papers. Barabás was a successful writer with good connections. And unlike József, who worked openly for the increasingly imperilled Wallenberg, his anti-Nazism took a secret form. Outwardly, he was a bona fide individual with an impressive track record of screenwriting for the Germans in Berlin. This would now stand him in good stead. But to whom could he turn? Only someone very influential could intervene on Vali's behalf with a monster like Péter Hain.

He got in touch with friends, colleagues, anyone who could be of assistance. His line was that Vali had been mistakenly arrested for hiding Jews, the police had no evidence against her and that it was absurd for such a celebrated and patently blameless person to be detained in the grim conditions of the Majestic.

They all agreed. But the problem was Péter Hain's inaccessibility. The man who had dared to filch from the booty of the Nazis wasn't inclined to be swayed by anyone. Barabás had to find and prevail upon somebody with access to the secret police chief. Eventually he came up with a possibility: Ferenc Fiala, press chief of the Arrow Cross government. Fiala was the most powerful figure in the newspaper world during the months of Szálasi's rule, and as a writer with close links to that world, Barabás had naturally encountered him already.

His first attempts to reach Fiala were unsuccessful. Days passed. At last he was able to speak to him on the telephone. He pleaded Vali's case. Here was a good Magyar, he argued, who was beyond reproach. She had taken part in countless charity concerts for the Hungarian Red Cross to aid wounded soldiers, war widows and war orphans. And she had sung so movingly to the troops at 'request' concerts that she had become their uncontested favourite (he mentioned the bundles of fan letters from the Front). He also spoke about her participation in Sztójay's 'Magyar Evening' in Berlin in 1943. Really, he insisted, a slight indignation creeping into his seeming deference, such a person deserved better treatment. Could he not use his influence on behalf of this innocent woman?

Fiala listened dispassionately to Barabás's appeal. Of course, this type of thing wasn't really his department. And he was a very busy man. But he was not altogether unsympathetic, and powerful people like to influence other powerful people. He told Barabás that, while he could make no promises, he would speak to Hain on his behalf. In due course, he said, Barabás would hear from him.

More days passed. Barabás grew extremely anxious. Could Fiala have forgotten? Or was it simply that his word was worthless? Should he call him again? He had to play it carefully. If he seemed too pushy or impatient, the press chief might become irate and decide not to co-operate at all. But meanwhile, precious time was being wasted. He worried about what was happening to Vali behind the impenetrable walls of the Majestic. For all he knew, they could be practising their usual brutal techniques on her.

At long last the awaited phone call came. Fiala seemed pleased with himself. He informed Barabás that he had finally got around to speaking to Hain, and as a result of his recommendation, Hain had agreed to listen to Barabás. He would make no promises, but the writer would at least be permitted to phone him and present his case. Fiala gave Barabás Hain's private number at the Majestic. The rest was up to him.

At ten o'clock on Tuesday morning, 5 December, Barabás dialled Hain's number.

The police chief answered the phone. His voice was relaxed.

Barabás spoke in an earnest, courteous manner. Again, he went through Vali's credentials as a patriotic Magyar, an unadulterated Christian, the troops' pin-up, star of charity concerts, etc. Hain listened in silence. Then Barabás heard some type of commotion in the background.

'Excuse me,' he said apologetically, 'am I interrupting something? If you have people there with you –'

'No, no,' answered Hain. 'It's just the birds making all this noise. You see, each morning at this time I have breakfast in bed, and the bluetits come to my window sill. I always throw them some crumbs from my tray. I'm very fond of these sweet little birds. There are lots of them in the woods here.'

Barabás saw his opportunity. An exceptionally well-read man, he began to quote to this ruthless henchman of Eichmann various passages from world literature about birds – the innocence, the beauty, the delights of our feathered friends. Hain was quite charmed, even moved.

Finally the conversation returned to the fate of Vali Rácz. Hain reflected for a moment, then sighed. 'All right. We'll let her go.'

Barabás could hardly believe it. He began to thank him profusely.

'There are some formalities,' Hain went on, 'which must be completed before her release. She will be ready to leave

78

tomorrow morning between ten and eleven.' He paused. 'And, Mr Barabás, do tell her not to get involved in this sort of thing again.'

The following morning, an overjoyed József drove his ambulance up to the top of Swabian Hill once again, to fetch Vali and take her home.

She had one final meeting with the young interrogator from Kaposvár. He glared at her as she stood before his desk. He wasn't at all pleased at his boss's whimsical decision to let her go. But he could do nothing, except to try one last time to frighten her into compliance. 'Just remember,' he said icily, 'we're going to keep a close eye on you. You'd better not step out of line again.'

Upstairs in the prisoners' room, Vali said goodbye to her friends. She gave away the few belongings that Karolin had brought for her – the blanket, the towel and the toiletries. She had grown especially close to Vera during those days and, as they were parting from each other, Vera removed a gold necklace with a heart-shaped pendant and pressed it into Vali's hand. She explained that it was the last precious thing she had, and she wanted Vali to look after it.

'It'll be safer with you,' said Vera.

Vali put on the necklace. 'I'll return it to you after the war.' The two women embraced. Then Vali went downstairs to where József was waiting.

Twenty minutes later she was at home. Karolin welcomed her tearfully and with open arms.

Vali had been strong and composed throughout the ten days of her ordeal; she attributed her self-control to the rigid discipline received at the hands of the nuns. But now that it was over she snapped and suffered a complete nervous collapse. All the tension and distress which had been building up inside was at last released and she fell to the floor in an uncontrollable fit of shaking and sobbing. It went on for a long time, while a desperate Karolin tried to console her. Her state was aggravated by anxiety over the fate of the five Jews she had been sheltering. Where could they have gone? Where could they hide?

When at length she quietened down, Karolin, alarmed at her

pallor and considerable loss of weight, encouraged her to eat. Afterwards she took a hot bath, and listened to the BBC which broadcast consoling news about the Germans' retreat.

That evening Barabás sent a car for her. She stayed overnight at his flat and heard the details of how he had engineered her release. In conclusion, he made a suggestion. 'Listen, Valikó, your life was entirely in this man's hands. He could have done with you as he wished. It might be a good idea to ring him up and thank him for setting you free. Here, give me your diary – I'll write his phone number into it.'

Vali took out the pocket diary which she always carried in her handbag and Barabás wrote down Hain's name and number. It was the worst thing he could have done.

As it turned out, Vali could never bring herself to call him. Just thinking about the man made her shudder. But the entry, in Barabás's hand, remained in her diary.

★

Twenty-four hours after Vali left the Majestic, all non-Jewish prisoners were taken away to begin another forced march westward. Few ever returned from it. And the day after that, the place was emptied of Jews. Like the proverbial rats deserting a sinking ship, the Gestapo and their Hungarian hirelings were preparing to get out of the city while they could. On the morning of 8 December, armed Arrow Cross militiamen operating under the murderous Father Kun entered the building and took all the Jews away. What happened to them after that would become known as one of the most heinous episodes of the war.

Eight

It was on 8 December, the same day that the Jewish prisoners at the Majestic were taken away, that the Red Army began its regular long-range bombardment of the capital. And so began the lengthy destruction of central Europe's most glittering capital.

That day also marked the completion of the exodus from Budapest of the Szálasi government – the Arrow Cross civil and military leadership set up their base at Sopron, as near as possible to their sponsors in the Reich. They regarded the move as a temporary necessity. Germany had promised reinforcements to defend the Hungarian capital, and what was more, it had boasted of its secret 'wonder weapons' which would devastate the advancing Russian forces. So Szálasi expected before long to re-enter the capital victorious. Not wishing to depend entirely on wonder weapons, though, he ordered the immediate conscription of all Hungarian males aged between fourteen and seventy, without exception.

This flight of the leadership stratum was to be a tragedy for thousands of Budapest Jews. Without the restraining influence of relatively civilized high-level individuals, total anarchy broke out amongst the Arrow Cross militia and the SS which had been left behind. Realizing that the end was at hand, the thugs took out their anger and frustrations on the hated Jews, torturing and murdering them wherever they could. These were the final crazed acts of a tyranny in its death throes. Jews were rounded up on the streets and dragged out of cellars and

81

'safe-houses'. Even Jewish hospitals and an orphanage were stormed and their inmates butchered. Countless Jews were shot in the nape of the neck and thrown into the Danube. (After the war hundreds of bodies were recovered from beside the broad pillars of the Elizabeth Bridge, which had prevented them from being carried downstream.)

Gangs of youths aged twelve or thirteen, many of them runaways from correctional institutions, roved through the city wearing Arrow Cross armbands and brandishing machine guns. Taking advantage of the prevailing chaos, they too became self-appointed executioners of the Jews.

The Zionist underground, which had been so active in saving lives through forging documents and establishing escape routes, could offer little armed resistance against the murderers. Almost all the Jewish men capable of bearing arms had been conscripted into the forced labour battalions, from which mass escape was impossible as there was no organized partisan movement for them to join. (Partisans could operate successfully in the mountainous terrain of Yugoslavia, but not in the open countryside of Hungary.) And so the majority of Jews in Budapest now were women, children, the elderly and the infirm.

The ghetto was often invaded by the rampaging thugs, and, unable to bury their dead, the survivors simply piled up their murdered friends and relatives in the streets and courtyards. A great number of the Jews living outside the ghetto had by now been forced into it, and its gates were closed on 10 December, sealing in some 70,000 inhabitants. The conditions inside were appalling – fifteen people were quartered in each room of each flat, with three or four to a bed. Starvation was the norm and medical aid was virtually nonexistent. There were still half as many again living outside the ghetto, in houses 'protected' by the neutral legations and the Red Cross, using forged papers or in hiding.

Himmler had on 25 November ordered an end to the further extermination and persecution of the Jews. But Eichmann proceeded to sabotage this order. At a meeting with Wallenberg, during which the Swede tried to convince him that he

82

would hang as a war criminal if he didn't stop the senseless massacre, Eichmann replied that he would do his job to the end, regardless. He finally fled the city on the evening of 23 December through the small gap still open to the West, and with only hours to spare before the Red Army closed its circle. Before his departure he made plans for the ghetto to be blown up, with the mass murder of all its inhabitants to be carried out by 500 German soldiers and 200 Hungarian policemen.

In this, however, he was thwarted by the ingenious Wallenberg, who, on learning of these plans, went to see August Schmidthuber, Commander of the Wehrmacht's *Feldherrnhalle* Division. Unlike Eichmann, Schmidthuber *did* care whether or not he was to hang, and Wallenberg's warning that he'd better not harm the Jews made the desired impression on him. Later, in January, when Schmidthuber was informed about the imminent destruction of the ghetto, he ordered it to be called off. Two days later it was liberated by Russian forces. In this way, Wallenberg has been credited with saving the population of the Budapest ghetto – the only wartime Jewish ghetto in Europe to escape obliteration. Schmidthuber, however, did not survive the war. He was killed during the Siege.

*

After her experiences at the Majestic, Vali was unable to face the prospect of returning to work at the Vidám Theatre. Her confidence had been undermined and she was still nervous and afraid about being watched by Hain's men. She had not forgotten the Kaposvár man's final words of warning. So she withdrew from all public activity and spent her days at home. It was then that a very strange incident took place.

A little further up Budakeszi Avenue there was a nursery where Vali often bought plants for her garden. And whenever she had some heavier gardening work to be done, the owner, Mr Kovács, would send his apprentice gardener to do it for her. János was a pleasant, helpful lad of about eighteen.

One day there was a ring at the gate and Vali found János standing there in a soldier's uniform bearing the fearsome insignia of the *Totenkopfverbände* – the 'death's head' division of the Waffen-SS. He greeted her with a wave and a grin.

'I'm passing by,' he explained. 'Thought I'd stop and say hello.'

'Well, János,' she said, warily, 'what have you done? Joined the army?'

'Yes, Miss Rácz.' He proudly displayed the rifle slung over his shoulder.

They spoke for a minute or two, then Vali had a thought. She had not left the house for several days and she was longing to take a long walk, have a change of scene. Only a couple of hundred yards up the road there was a pathway leading into a large forest. In the past Vali had often walked there, but lately she had no desire to go alone. Now she asked János whether he cared to accompany her for an hour or so.

'I've got to return to the barracks now,' he told her, 'but I won't be there long. I can return later this afternoon. Then I would be happy to escort you through the forest.'

As he promised, János returned later that day. Vali put on a warm coat and some boots, and together they walked up Budakeszi Avenue to the forest. János whistled, proud now not only about his smart new uniform, but to be in the company of such a famous lady.

Vali delighted in the cold, sharp air of the forest and its deep silence. They heard only the birds and their own footsteps. The walk was doing her good. Her spirits rose and her mood became playful.

'Do you know how to use that rifle of yours?' she asked the young SS soldier.

'Of course,' he answered.

'Show it to me.'

János took the weapon off his shoulder and handed it to her. 'Please be careful with it, though.'

Vali examined the rifle, then raised it and peered through the range-finder. 'How do I shoot?'

János unlocked the safety-catch and told her what to do. She took aim at a distant tree and pulled the trigger. The blast echoed through the vast, silent forest. Vali and the teenager laughed. Then she handed the rifle back to him and they walked on.

A few minutes later they came upon a middle-aged man wearing the typical clothes of a woodsman. He introduced himself as the local forest ranger and asked what the shooting had been about. János explained that Miss Rácz, wishing to try out his rifle, had fired it in fun. The ranger made a disapproving face.

'Are there many animals in this forest?' Vali asked him.

'Foxes, a lot of rabbits and some deer.'

A little later, when they had parted from the ranger and were heading back towards Budakeszi Avenue, Vali turned suddenly to her escort.

'Listen, János, I have an idea. You know how difficult it has become to get food, especially meat. Perhaps, when you have the time, you could come here and shoot a rabbit for me. I would pay you, naturally.'

Again, the young man was obliging. He said he would return the next day when he was off-duty, and bring the rabbit to her house as soon as he'd shot it.

János left Vali at her front gate. She thanked him and they agreed to meet the following day. She was pleased. Karolin could make them a good stew from the rabbit. After all, it had been a common dish during the winter months in Gölle.

But János never showed up with the rabbit. Two, three days went by. Vali presumed that the army must have stationed him elsewhere. Or perhaps he'd tried to kill a rabbit but wasn't a very good shot.

Then she heard the sad news going around the neighbourhood. Someone had found János's body in the forest. He'd been shot at close range and had been dead for some days.

★

In mid-December the region of the Dunántúl fell to the Russians, and Vali was cut off from her parents in Gölle. They could send her no more parcels of food. It would be many weeks before they had news of each other, during which time the fate of their country was decided.

Lajos Esküdt slipped out of Gölle just before the Russians arrived. Travelling up to the capital was a challenge, as the transportation system had all but broken down. But somehow, through a combination of horse-drawn cart and the odd train, he managed to reach his flat on the outskirts of Budapest. There he found the message Karolin had left for him and soon he was reunited with his wife at Vali's house. The war had done nothing to improve his nerves.

Another new occupant was introduced by Zsóka. Once more the housekeeper called upon Vali's compassion and generosity, explaining that her niece from Transylvania, young Marika, had been made homeless by the war and had nowhere to go. She would make herself useful and help with the chores, Zsóka assured her employer. What Zsóka omitted to tell anyone was the reason for Marika's plight: the relative with whom she'd been staying in Budapest was an Arrow Cross big shot who'd been forced to flee to Germany before the Russians arrived.

And so Marika duly moved in – a full-bodied blonde peasant girl whose gold teeth glinted when she smiled. She never did prove to be terribly helpful with the chores, but was soon to reveal her true talent: making the randy Red Army happy.

One night about fifty German soldiers – reinforcements sent from the Reich to help defend the capital – were billeted at Vali's house. They were a courteous and quiet group who lay on the floor of the sitting room with their heads on their kit bags. They all seemed sad and contemplative, as if they already knew it was a lost battle, a lost war. They were to be among the final sacrifices to Hitler's madness.

During these last days before the Russians' circle around the city closed completely, Vali managed to make one or two expeditions to Swabian peasant villages to the west of Budapest in search of food for her household. Once a friend, a young concert organizer from Budapest, drove her in his car to a village not far from Székesfehérvár, where they were able to buy flour, fresh eggs, and even two live chickens, which Vali carried in a basket.

As they were about to begin the journey home, the sky was suddenly alive with the roar of Russian bombers. Vali and her companion dropped to the ground as fire-bombs fell all around them. She was still clutching the basket with the chickens and the panic-stricken birds now squawked loudly and struggled to escape. The raid went on for several minutes. At last, they decided to wait no longer. The planes still thundering overhead, they threw the chickens in the car, jumped in after them, and sped off furiously in the direction of the capital.

Romeo and Piroska closed down for good on 23 December. Mihály Szüle's half-Jewish wife was denounced, and so the couple went into hiding in the cellar of the house of a famous Hungarian dramatic actress, Mária Lázár. The Szüles were to spend the entire two-month Siege in that cellar, being looked after by Mária.

Her house was in one of the elegant cobblestoned streets on top of Castle Hill. This is the medieval heart of Buda where, in the eighteenth century, Hungarian noblemen built their grand, yellow-stuccoed houses or 'little palaces', with their towering portals and inner courtyards.

Beneath this whole Castle district is a vast subterranean labyrinth of inter-connecting tunnels and chambers, believed to have been built by the Turks during their occupation in the sixteenth and seventeenth centuries. Mária's cellar was also part of this extraordinary and complex maze. Throughout the Szüles' period of hiding there, they were unaware that Mária was also sheltering a hundred Jewish children in a neighbouring cellar. When, during the height of the Siege, food became unobtainable, she kept them from starvation by cooking meals out of the carcasses of horses found on the streets.

Neither did Mihály and his wife know that, when the German army retreated to the Castle as its final stronghold before capitulation, it set up its dressing station for wounded soldiers in another one of these cellars, very close to theirs. Many soldiers, trying to escape from the battle zone via these tunnels, either lost their way or became trapped when the Russians sealed up some of the entrances. Their skeletons were discovered long after the war.

Also on 23 December the new, multi-party Hungarian Provisional Government declared war on Germany. The government had been set up in the city of Debrecen, in northeastern Hungary, and had held the first session of its National

87

Assembly two days earlier.

At mid-morning on the 24th, Paul Barabás's thirteen-year-old son, Károly, stopped briefly at 47d Budakeszi Avenue to deliver his father's present for Vali, as the following day was not only Christmas but her birthday. The boy didn't come in because he was in a hurry; he told Karolin at the door that he was due to meet his father at the bottom of the Avenue. Paul had meanwhile gone up to his flat on Rose Hill to retrieve some important papers. He had moved out temporarily, as it was in the thick of the battle zone, and Károly explained that he and his parents were staying at the home of a friend, further away, in a safer part of Buda. Vali wondered why Barabás didn't bring the present himself that evening, as he was expected for dinner.

And so, on Christmas Eve, Budapest was enclosed. The remaining German and Hungarian soldiers were trapped and, unbeknownst to them, it would no longer be possible for the promised reinforcements from the Wehrmacht to get through the Russian lines. The great Siege, the 'Fortress Budapest' tactic ordered by Hitler, was about to begin. All day there were shots and explosions on Budakeszi Avenue and in the surrounding area. It was impossible for anyone to leave Vali's house. A small German bomb demolished one of the stone gateposts of the house, making it impossible to close the gate.

At dusk Vali saw the first Russian soldiers making their way down the Avenue to the bottom where it merged with the street called Olasz Fasor (which means 'Italian row of trees'). There the troops stopped. This was the new Front Line.

She watched from her bedroom window as, gradually, more and more soldiers sat down on the low wall beside the railing which bordered her front garden. Ten, then fifteen, then twenty men. Finally she counted nearly thirty. In the growing darkness, in their dark uniforms, they looked like a row of great, silent birds, sitting, waiting on a garden fence.

Vali guessed what it meant. The troops were stopping here for the night. They required billets. Hastily, she displayed several of her film placards and publicity photographs around the sitting room. The Russians, by tradition, were very fond of singers, actors, musicians. It might help her to make her profession immediately obvious to them.

She had also been garnering a few essential Russian words, writing them phonetically into a little notebook which she carried around with her. She believed in being prepared for the inevitable.

And in a crazy act of self-defence, if worse came to worst, she still had her father's old First World War service pistol. She'd brought it back from Gölle years ago, when she first moved into the house and felt vulnerable at night, a woman surrounded only by other women. This she now placed into the pocket of her dress. She'd heard about the brutality of the Russian soldiers. Had the gun been found on her person, she would most certainly have been shot herself.

After a while the Russians rose wearily to their feet. The front gate was ajar and so the troops, led by the officer in charge, started walking in single file down the pathway to the house. But before they could knock on the front door, Vali had flung it open. With a broad smile and outstretched arms, she cried, '*Tovarish*!'

Nine

Like true, long-lost comrades, Vali and the officer embraced. Then he and the other Russians entered the house, looked around and saw all the film placards. '*Aktrisa*,' they said to each other, nodding with approval. The scene was something that they could understand and identify with: even in Stalinist Russia the celebrated actress in her *dacha* was an acceptable social concept. Had she been the wife of a rich banker or businessman, on the other hand, inhabiting one of the grand mansions of the neighbourhood, the reaction would have been very different. With cries of 'Dirty *kapitalist*!' those homes were looted and vandalized, and the women found in them raped. On that same evening an elderly, rich widow who lived nearby was literally raped to death by a gang of marauding Russian soldiers.

The officer made it obvious that he wanted to billet his men there for the night. The soldiers looked exhausted, and sat down wherever they could on the sitting-room floor. Karolin, with her usual sensitivity in difficult matters, hastily prepared something for them to eat and drink. Zsóka helped. And her buxom niece pottered about, displaying a gold-toothed grin which the Russians found most fetching.

The atmosphere in the house was subdued, but Vali and Karolin were still apprehensive. After all, the ground floor had never been wall-to-wall Red Army and they didn't know what to expect. So, a little later on that Christmas Eve, to induce a spirit of seasonal goodwill amongst the assembled atheists, Vali sat down at the baby grand in front of the blacked-out window and sang traditional Hungarian Christmas songs for them. Once again, as at the Majestic, her singing was her only refuge, and the best antidote to anxiety.

Outside the war raged. They could hear distant explosions and the closer sound of gunfire; the Russians were firing into the centre of the capital and the besieged Germans were firing outwards. But the soldiers sat or lay on the floor in total silence, obviously moved and even mesmerized by the exotic woman at the piano. They were lulled into a sense of peace and safety.

But it was a false one. The spell was broken when all of a sudden, in the middle of a song, a stray bullet crashed through the window behind Vali, whizzed past her head and embedded itself in one of the soldiers. There was a commotion. He was taken away at once to their army medical team stationed nearby.

Barabás didn't turn up for dinner, as expected. Vali assumed that, unable to make his way through the dangerous turmoil of the streets, he'd been forced to remain indoors somewhere. It was better that way, she concluded, feeling instinctively that the Russians were more kindly disposed towards her as a vulnerable, unattached female. Barabás's presence would only have aroused antipathy and suspicion amongst them.

She still worried, when she went up to bed, that sometime during the night she might find uninvited visitors in her bedroom. But the respectful troops stayed downstairs.

Christmas morning saw a lot of activity on Budakeszi Avenue. The Russians were moving in their heavy artillery. In the back yard of Mr Kovács's nursery they set up one of their famed 'Stalin Organs' (which were, incidentally, made in Tennessee and supplied to Mr Stalin by the Americans). This ear-splitting rocket launcher's nickname was due to the row of tall, upturned barrels resembling the pipes of an organ.

It was bustling at 47d, too, as the troops prepared to leave the night's billet and move on. It was about half-past ten, and Vali was upstairs, still in her dressing gown, playing some of her records.

At last the soldiers departed, leaving the door open behind them. It was quiet. The other members of the household were either in the basement or the kitchen. And no one noticed three men walk down the pathway and enter the house.

All at once the record on the turntable in Vali's bedroom slowed down and ground to a halt. She tried but couldn't get the record player to work again. Fearing a possible power failure, she tried the radio, then the light switch. Everything was dead. Disheartened, she got down on her knees to tidy away the records which lay on the floor, and which she had been sorting through that morning.

She was still on the floor, putting the records into a neat stack, when she heard a sound in the room and was suddenly aware that she was no longer alone. She turned around and the first thing she saw, immediately behind her, was a pair of high-quality black leather boots. Lifting her eyes she saw a black leather coat, and her gaze followed it upwards until she reached an attractive, smiling face, and the cap of a high-ranking Red Army officer.

Beside the officer stood two of his aides, one of whom was an interpreter who now stepped forward and explained to Vali that the colonel wished to establish his quarters in her home.

The colonel reached out a hand to help Vali up. 'Would that be possible?' he asked courteously, in Russian.

Vali understood his words. She took his hand and stood up. 'Yes,' she replied, a faint but promising smile on her lips, 'yes, it is possible.'

They went downstairs. The colonel wanted the small front room for himself. As it was just off the entrance hall, he could come and go easily. The Esküdts, who had been sleeping there, would have to move upstairs.

Vali studied this strangely appealing new member of the household. He was of medium height, strong and well-built, with dark hair and warm brown eyes. The colonel, for his part, knew precisely what he would find in Vali's bedroom before he entered it; he'd already seen the photos and film posters in the sitting room. And he liked what he saw. He left the house now, to return only in the evening.

There was good news and bad news on that Christmas Day, Vali's thirty-third birthday.

The good news was that when the colonel returned that night he and Vali plunged into what would be a most propitious love affair. And from then on he was referred to, simply, as Sasha.

The bad news was that Vali was right about the power failure. A well-aimed bomb had demolished the local power station, leaving that part of Budapest without electricity. It would be months, and the war would be over, before the lights went on once more at 47d Budakeszi Avenue.

★

Right up until then the inhabitants of Budapest had been carrying on as far as possible with their normal daily lives. Despite the frequent air raids by Russian bombers, the constant shelling from the city outskirts, the martial-law decrees and the savage domination of the Arrow Cross, the Budapesters remained unintimidated. They went to their offices, shopped, frequented cafés, bars, restaurants, places of entertainment, advertised their services in the papers: 'Masseuse with extensive experience, will come to your home. Replies to be marked "French degree-holder" .' (From *Magyarország-Pest*, 20 December.)

But now all this changed. On 27 December a curfew was brought in, forbidding civilians to be out on the streets between 5 p.m. and 7 a.m. On the same day all the city's cinemas and theatres were closed down. The populace was battening down the hatches in preparation for the storm which was brewing around them.

On the 29th, over loudspeakers, the Soviet High Command issued an ultimatum to the general in command of the German and Hungarian forces defending the city. In return for their unconditional surrender, the Soviets promised to allow their German POWs to return home after the war, to let their Hungarian captives go free after questioning and verification, to give medical attention to the wounded and to allow all soldiers to retain their uniforms and valuables.

Two Soviet envoys, Steinmetz and Ostapenko, were dispatched behind German lines to deliver personally the written ultimatum. Steinmetz never made it: he died when his car drove

93

over a land mine. Ostapenko, however, did manage to reach the headquarters of the 8th SS mounted division under the command of SS-General Ruhmor. Without even reading it, Ruhmor rejected the ultimatum and sent the envoy away. On his way back to the Russian positions, while still in no man's land, he came under Russian fire and was killed by mistake.

The Soviets used the death of the envoys as valuable propaganda, claiming that they were murdered by the Wehrmacht. It gave them an excuse to escalate the fierceness of their assault.

Aiming their 'Stalin Organs' straight at the heart of their foe, the Red Army unleashed its might upon Budapest. The Siege had begun.

*

It soon became clear to Vali just how lucky she was to have Sasha as the 'guardian angel' of 47d. Once it became known that Vali was the woman of a Red Army colonel (and a member of the General Staff, to boot), her house was strictly off-limits to the more barbaric of the Russian invaders.

What's more, Sasha and his ever-present aides supplied the household with all kinds of otherwise unobtainable items. As soon-to-be victors in a vanquished land, they raided the city's warehouses and private stores, often returning in the evening with their spoils: bottles of wine and champagne, tinned goods, provisions, the odd pig shot on sight and loaded into the jeep.

Russian soldiers were not so well fed by their army as the Americans with their 'K-rations'. They took what they needed for themselves and their horses from the lands they invaded. The rest of their food was supplied by the US. When one of the Russians later billeted at her house gave Vali a tin of vegetables, she peeled the Russian label off to reveal an American one underneath.

Unbeknownst to Vali, her parents' house in Gölle was also being used as a Russian billet. Their Russians, however, were not very friendly or generous. Far from supplying the Ráczes with anything, they merely helped themselves to whatever they needed. The headmaster and his wife were compelled to hide their foodstuffs in the larder and conceal its door behind a heavy cabinet, or they would have had nothing left.

Sasha grew very fond of kind, motherly Aunt Karolin, who spoke to him sweetly in Hungarian, as if he could understand, and cooked wonderful meals for everyone from the bounty brought back by his men. And in true Russian style, he always greeted her with a kiss full on the lips. He did this one evening while Lajos was sitting nearby. The furious husband jumped to his feet.

'Did you see that?' he cried out to Vali. 'I knew it! He's having an affair with her!'

Vali waved him aside. 'Sit down, you fool. He's having an affair with *me*.'

Sasha's driver and some of the others in his entourage paid frequent visits to Marika's room in the basement. The busty blonde, who hadn't realized that a siege could be such fun, was only too willing to oblige. The fact that Zsóka also slept in the basement was not overlooked and the Transylvanian house-keeper, too, revealed her hidden talents. It was all happening at 47d.

Often in the evenings Vali would play the piano and sing to Sasha and other off-duty officers who came to visit him at the house. The sitting room was now too cold for such gatherings, though. The window shattered by a bullet on Christmas Eve could only be inadequately boarded up, and without electricity there was no central heating. So, unable to use the baby grand, Vali had the small upright brought down from upstairs and put into the room occupied by Sasha, which was warmed by a small wood- and coal-burning stove. And there, relaxing with drinks in their hands, the Red Army officers were entertained by the *chanteuse*.

When the word spread that there was a civilized officer living at Vali's house, local people sometimes came to seek his help. One day a distraught Jesuit priest arrived at the door. He explained that the Jesuit church around the corner in Labanc Street had been overrun by Russian soldiers who, with their inevitable scorn for religion, were stabling their horses in the *manréz*, the hall used by the priests for spiritual meditation. When the priests protested, they were threatened and abused.

95

Sasha shook his head and looked doubtful. Knowing the extent of the aversion for Christianity inherent in Soviet dogma, he didn't think he could help. But he promised to look into the matter. And, in the end, through his intervention, the Jesuits regained their *manréz* and were able to carry on (at least for the time being) unmolested.

As the Siege progressed, the infrastructure of the capital was gradually demolished. The power stations, gasworks, telephone exchanges and municipal waterworks were blown up. Nothing was spared. In the exceptionally cold winter of 1944-5, people cowered in their homes without warmth, light, food or communication . . . and in constant fear for their lives.

The occupants of Vali's house were tormented by the multi-barrelled rocket launcher positioned in the Kovács' nursery up the street. Its angle of projection was such that the rockets, fired directly overhead, only narrowly cleared the roof, making everyone fearful and apprehensive lest the roof be blown off. All day the rockets soared and screeched, bombarding the German positions. The walls trembled. Vali and the others, including the sheepdog, Juliska (who by now had grown quite used to the sounds of war), spent more and more time sheltering in the basement.

Small stoves were hastily set up wherever it was possible to knock a hole into the chimney-breast for a flue. But fuel had to be used sparingly – like everything else, it was in very short supply.

When the nearby waterworks were destroyed and there was no more running water, Zsóka and her niece fetched it daily from the large municipal well up the hill. It was a hazardous undertaking, carrying the heavy buckets back and forth while shells exploded and gunfire criss-crossed the city.

On 13 January, after three weeks of ceaseless bombardment, the Russians entered Pest, and that was when things really began to get too hot for the Germans. Unable to maintain their positions, they were forced further and further back, towards the Danube. And on the night of the 17th, as the Red Army at last reached and liberated the Jewish ghetto, Hitler reluctantly consented to the abandonment of Pest. The Wehrmacht retreated across the river to Buda, blowing up the remaining bridges behind them. Fleeing on their coat-tails were the bands of Arrow Cross fanatics that even the Nazis despised. For another month they were to carry on with their frenzied programme of murder in Buda.

It was at this point that the Swedish hero, Raoul Wallenberg, disappeared into the hands of the Soviet authorities. Up until the day of Pest's liberation, even though he himself was often forced to take refuge at the International Red Cross headquarters, he continued to go out on rescue missions, saving Jews about to be massacred by the Arrow Cross. But on 17 January he was driven away by Russian officers, ostensibly to be questioned by the commander of the Russian forces in Debrecen. He went with them willingly and even hopefully, because he was eager to put before the Russians his detailed proposals for the care and rehabilitation of the Jewish survivors of Budapest.

But he never reached Debrecen. The Soviets were deeply suspicious of Wallenberg's actions and motives in Hungary. Their inherent cynicism, coupled with paranoia, led them to conclude that the young member of one of Sweden's foremost capitalist families was no mere altruist, but that he must have been working as a spy for the United States. He was never seen or heard of again in the free world. Many years later, though, reports reached the West of sightings of Wallenberg in various Soviet prisons. As no proven official explanation of his fate has ever been forthcoming, it is conceivable that he is still languishing in one today.

After they relinquished Pest, the hilltop Castle in Buda became the Germans' stronghold; from there they made their last, desperate and futile stand. They still believed what their High Command had told them – that it would not be long before German reinforcements broke through the Russian lines to come to their aid. And indeed, at the beginning of January a Waffen-SS division led by SS-General Gille had set off towards Budapest for this purpose. But General Tolbuchin's Third Ukrainian Front was dispatched from its area of operation, Transdanubia, to cut off the German division. Only twenty kilometres from the Hungarian capital, the two armies engaged. The German advance was successfully repelled.

For weeks the Germans had been running out of supplies. Now they were in dire need of ammunition, fuel, medicaments and food if they were to continue to defend the city. At first, they'd been able to receive supplies by air, but once the racecourse in Pest had fallen to the Russians, the Luftwaffe had no suitable landing spot within the city. They were forced to drop supplies by parachute.

Another plan was to reach the besieged troops by water. A forty-ton boat loaded with fuel and ammunition tried to approach Budapest along the Danube, but it ran aground before it got there. Some crew members later managed, under cover of darkness, to transport the vital cargo into the city on small boats.

The disillusioned Hungarian troops were deserting their posts in droves. Some donned civilian clothes and escaped the city, others surrendered to the Soviets and still others formed a fighting regiment under the Red Army and turned on their former allies. This further lowered the spirits of the Germans, who, on their daily diet of a bowl of horsemeat soup and 150 grammes of bread, were already deeply demoralized. By now, there were over 5,000 wounded soldiers in the underground dressing station so close to the cellars where the Szüles and the Jewish children were hiding.

The liberated ghetto in Pest was a sight as unspeakable as the concentration camps. It was a scene of misery and starvation, disease and carnage. There were corpses everywhere – in the apartments, in basements and courtyards, on the streets and pavements. The living had become inured to the sight and stench of the decomposing dead: men, women and children who had fallen victim to both the Nazis and the Arrow Cross, the bombing, shelling and street-fighting.

Now the rest crawled out of their wretched holes and their freezing cellars, and found that they had, miraculously, survived. They may have been themselves half-dead, but they were also half-alive. So they began to piece together what was left, to construct life anew. And with all their tragedies and hardships, they were still to be counted amongst the most fortunate Jews in Europe, for theirs was the one ghetto still extant.

On 20 January, representatives of the Hungarian Provisional Government set up in Debrecen a month earlier went to Moscow, where they concluded an armistice treaty with the Allies. With Pest now under the apparent control of the new government, retribution was not long in coming. The Budapest People's Court was convened immediately and the first trial was held at the end of January in the only venue suitable at the time – the large auditorium of the Music Academy. It was a very cold winter and the auditorium was unheated; everyone sat in overcoats. On the same stage where a decade earlier Vali had received her diploma from Ernő Dohnányi, the first two Hungarian war criminals to be tried now received their death sentences.

Szívós and Rotyis were two military guards in charge of forced labour units, fascist henchmen who had between them killed 124 Jewish labour servicemen and tormented countless others. They were sentenced to be hanged in public from street lamps in the Oktogon, the large octagonal square in the middle of Andrássy Avenue. The sentence was carried out on a frosty morning at the beginning of February. A large crowd gathered in the square to watch the hanging. The ropes were too thin and when Rotyis was hanged his rope snapped. They had to string him up again. When the two were finally declared dead the frenzied crowd began to cheer and to beat the bodies with their fists or whatever they had in their hands. Then the Germans opened fire on the square from the Castle across the river, and the people quickly dispersed. The two bodies, however, were left hanging there for weeks.

Although justice was being carried out under the banner of the legitimate Hungarian Government, the newly arrived Hungarian Muscovites, loyal only to Stalin, had already put into motion the machinery with which they would eventually assume total control of the country. And the names of Gábor Péter, Zoltán Vas and Ernő Gerő, instrumental in establishing this 'People's Court', would one day be as synonymous with terror and death as the names of the most murderous villains of the Arrow Cross.

*

The feelings between Vali and her protector, Sasha, deepened over the weeks that he stayed with her. This did not mean, though, that he didn't have her politically vetted. At that time everyone had to prove his or her innocence. She was interviewed more than once by the Soviet authorities, first in Buda and then later, after the Siege was over, in Pest. Sasha also made his own discreet inquiries into her background. For all he knew, she could have had an equally ardent affair with some member of the Nazi top brass during the Occupation. But he soon satisfied himself that she was beyond reproach.

One evening, soon after the liberation of Pest, Vali answered a knock at the door to find a Hungarian Communist worker with an anxious expression, cap in hand. He asked to speak to the Russian colonel billeted there. Sasha was in his small front room, as usual, and came out at once to see the visitor.

The worker, who spoke fluent Russian, told them of his predicament. After several years' activity in the Communist underground, he had finally been able to emerge from his secret existence. Now he was eager to join his old comrades, but he was in Buda and they were in Pest, and all the bridges had been destroyed. His only hope of crossing the river was by boat. Could the colonel help him to reach the other side?

Sasha promised to get him on to one of the Russian military boats plying the river by night. The worker cheered up and expressed his gratitude to the Red Army officer. He was given a glass of wine, and, before he disappeared again into the black night, Sasha took him aside and the two men spoke for a few minutes in quiet, earnest tones. The subject of their informal discussion was Vali. Again, Sasha asked about her affiliations, her sympathies and activities. The Hungarian could say nothing against her. She had appeared for a few weeks in an innocent play, but had otherwise kept a low profile during the Occupation. Unlike some others in the world of the arts, she'd made no public pro-German proclamations, she had not been

100

involved in any propaganda.

Sasha was pleased. That night he was more passionate than ever.

As Vali's Russian vocabulary increased, she was able to ask more questions of her own. She talked to Sasha about his life in the Soviet Union. He told her about Moscow and the Black Sea resorts where he spent his holidays. He wasn't eager to give away too many details. He admitted that he had a wife and Vali liked to imagine her as the archetypal thick-limbed Russian woman, wearing a *babushka* and no make-up. He never said much about his wife and gave the impression that he was pleased to be away from her, and that in fact he was rather enjoying the war. How else could he have had this opportunity to travel abroad, not to speak of other things . . .?

He was kind to Vali and the others in her house. He gave her a sense of security in a dangerous world, and she was even able to enjoy rare feasts in a time of terrible deprivation. She could have asked for nothing more. And if she didn't love him, what did it matter? Her feelings for him were almost as deep.

Inevitably, though, the time came for him to move on. In late January Sasha received orders to take his troops southeast into another arena of ferment, Rumania, where the local Communists, instructed by Moscow, were poised to seize power. (General Sanatescu, leader of the coalition government, had already been ousted, and now his successor General Radescu was about to go the same way because of his conflicts with the Soviet authorities. The following month the Communists staged mass demonstrations in Bucharest and stormed the Ministry of Internal Affairs. The cabinet was forced to resign, thus marking the end of Rumania's brief period of self-determination. Now the country's Sovietization began in earnest.)

Sasha promised Vali that he would return to Budapest as soon as he could, and told her not to worry. He would arrange for his quarters to be passed on only to carefully chosen officers of the Red Army, who would continue to protect her (although not, perhaps, in quite the same manner). And in the event of the house being temporarily unoccupied by these 'guardians', he

101

left an impressive-looking notice in Russian for her to post on the front door. It read: 'This is a protected house and entry is forbidden – by order of the Soviet Military Authorities.'

Sasha fulfilled his promise. Almost as soon as he left, a quiet, middle-aged captain, a schoolteacher in civilian life, moved into his place. He was so unassuming that Vali barely knew he was there. Although he couldn't have been more different from Sasha, he seemed equally effective as a deterrent to the savages.

But the captain didn't stay long. And it was during the short interlude before the next lot arrived that Vali received her nocturnal visit from a lecherous Mongolian. She'd put the notice up on the door, but it had little effect in this case. The broad, bull-necked soldier, having heard of the *aktrisa* who lived there, muscled his way into the house with obviously lewd intentions. It was late. The others were asleep. So Vali found herself alone with the wild-eyed, pock-marked Mongolian. She showed him into the front room.

'Please sit down,' she said lightly, trying to mask her alarm. 'I'll bring you a drink, and then I'll play a little music for you.'

He stared at her, breathing heavily. But he went along with the suggestion and plonked down into an armchair.

She played the piano and sang for him for a long time. She told him about Sasha, referring to him as her 'fiancé' and emphasizing the fact that he was a colonel and a member of the General Staff. Meanwhile the Mongolian drank a lot, and the more he drank the harder he stared and the heavier he breathed. He was clearly finding it difficult to restrain himself. At last he seemed to be fairly bursting with lust, his dark eyes glowing in his great round face.

Vali was tired and frightened in equal measure. The soldier seemed ready to leap on her at any moment. She had to defuse the situation. Once again, she fell back on her instincts. Calmly, gently, she closed the lid of the piano.

'It's very late.' She smiled apologetically. 'Please go now.'

His breath had become wheezy, but still he peered at her in silent desire. Was it better or worse for him to be drunk? Vali wondered anxiously. Then, after a moment or two, he let out a deep, long sigh and rose unsteadily to his feet. He bowed his

102

head slightly, then headed towards the door.

And that was the end of that.

It never happened again. Within a couple of days Fyodor and Nadjuska arrived to take up quarters at 47d, and they proved to be both kind and caring. Nadjuska was a nurse attached to the Red Army, and Fyodor, a moustachioed, fur-hatted Cossack, was a veterinarian looking after the army's horses. They were lovers and had arranged to occupy the billet together.

They were impressed by Vali's effortless use of their language, which she put down to the constant phonetic scribblings in her ubiquitous notebook. She had had to master it, she explained, for her own protection. And Sasha had been very helpful in broadening her vocabulary.

'It seems most unlikely that she could have learnt the language so quickly,' Fyodor told Nadjuska one day while Vali was within earshot. 'Perhaps she is really a spy!'

Vali listened to his words with trepidation. But Nadjuska excoriated him for his impertinent remark, telling him to retract it at once. And the Cossack never referred to spies again.

They were generally out during the day, and on one occasion Vali found herself in urgent need of their protection. A Russian boy, not more than twelve years old, had entered the house unseen and gone down into the basement. The next thing Vali knew, he had brought up her bicycle and was pushing it through the kitchen, heading for the front door.

(It was commonplace for boys of that age to accompany the Red Army wherever it went. Often the sons of soldiers, they were used for various purposes – to run errands and carry messages, to squeeze through tight spaces where a grown man would not fit or to carry out tasks for which a uniformed soldier would be dangerously conspicuous.)

At a time when there was no public transportation in the city and private cars and taxis were virtually non-existent, a bicycle was an invaluable piece of property. The boy thought so, too.

Vali barred his way. 'Stop! You can't have that!'

He pulled a revolver out of his belt and aimed it at her, his finger already on the trigger.

'Lajos, come quickly!' Vali called to her uncle, who was at

that moment descending the stairs.

Lajos hurried to her side and confronted the young intruder. 'I'll get behind him and force his arm down,' he told Vali through clenched teeth, 'then you can grab the gun.'

'No! He might pull the trigger first and shoot me!'

But the stubborn old man, who'd been used to bad times for years, was not about to give in to an adolescent thief, whether or not he was armed. He began to grapple with him.

Vali cried out in alarm. Lajos could easily be killed. And if he happened to shoot the boy, intentionally or by accident, they would probably both be finished off by the Soviets.

'Let him go!' she yelled frantically. 'Let him take the bicycle!'

Reluctantly, Lajos loosened his grip and stepped backwards. He and the boy glared fiercely at each other for a moment, then the Russian took his prize and left.

That evening a despairing Vali related the episode to Nadjuska.

'This should never have happened,' said the nurse. 'I will see what I can do about it tomorrow.'

The following evening Nadjuska returned with the bicycle. The thief had not been difficult to track down as he was attached to her own battalion. 'I gave him a really good scolding,' she said with satisfaction. 'Perhaps I should have spanked him, as well!'

★

By the first week of February the Germans defending the Castle, led by SS-General Pfeffer-Wildenbruch, at last faced the grim fact that no reinforcements would be coming to their aid. With the fall of the only other German stronghold, the Citadella on top of Gellért Hill a little further to the south, all their hopes evaporated. From the Citadella the Russians were now able to fire directly into the Castle.

So, on the morning of 11 February Pfeffer-Wildenbruch at last decided to act. He informed his General Staff that on that evening at 8 p.m. they would attempt to break out of the Castle, penetrate the Russian lines and escape into the nearby wooded hills to the west, whence they would head towards their own lines in western Hungary. The break-out would succeed only if it took the enemy completely by surprise. In order to maintain secrecy, the plan would be withheld from the troops until the last minute.

At precisely 8 p.m. on 11 February 1945, some 20,000 German troops, plus an additional few thousand Hungarian soldiers (together with many wives and children), streamed through the Castle's Viennese Gate and down the hill to Széna Square. They were armed with rifles and machine guns. But as they approached the Olasz Fasor, which led up into Budakeszi Avenue, they came under the merciless fire of Russian rockets and mortars. Only 758 of them ever reached the German positions. The rest were either killed or captured. As it later transpired, the Russians had known of the exact time of the break-out and had been lying in wait.

All night long the battle raged and the morning light revealed a scene of horror: what had been a pleasant tree-lined street was transformed into a smouldering ruin, covered with the corpses of soldiers and civilians, women and children.

SS-General Pfeffer-Wildenbruch took a different escape route from the great mass of soldiers. He was aware that from the labyrinth of tunnels under the Castle there was a passage leading to a spot beyond the Russian line of attack and within easy reach of the woods of Buda. He and a few of his men made their way stealthily along this tunnel. But when they emerged from it at the other end they were greeted by machine-gun fire. The well-informed Russians had been waiting for them, too. The General was taken captive and led before his Russian counter-part, General Malinovsky of the Second Ukrainian Front.

Malinovsky was furious with him. 'If I wasn't obliged to account for your head,' he ranted, 'I'd be most happy to have you hanged in the courtyard of the Castle!'

His fury was understandable. The fifty-one days of the Siege had tied down eight Russian divisions, a thousand aircraft and a vast amount of heavy artillery. The Second and Third Ukrainian Fronts were weakened by their losses. Hitler's 'Fortress Budapest' had prolonged the war not only in Hungary, but in Europe as a whole, by slowing down the Red Army's progress towards Austria and Germany.

As for the city of Budapest and its people, neither the Germans nor the Russians had bothered to spare them. The two great armies had, with a ruthless disregard, fought out their bloody battle to the end, and in the process one of the finest cities of the world was ruined. Only a quarter of its buildings remained intact, its eight beautiful bridges lay in the water, and its showpiece – the Castle – was reduced to rubble. And 20,000 Hungarian civilians had been killed. Neither did Ferenc Szálasi, the 'Leader of the Nation', ever have his own people's interests at heart. He had all along served only the Reich.

In contrast to this destruction, the other Habsburg capital, Vienna, emerged from the war relatively unscathed. The city which had seven years earlier given Hitler his most ecstatic welcome, was relinquished by the Germans after a minor struggle lasting only seven days. It was made to suffer much less for its allegiances; perhaps that is why, even today, it is full of old people who speak of the 'good old Hitler times'.

★

On the evening of the Germans' break-out attempt, the Russians had positioned a cannon in Vali's back garden in preparation for the big event. Everyone in the house, aware that a battle was about to ensue very close at hand, went down to seek shelter in the basement.

At first there was an unearthly silence. It was quieter than at any time since the Siege began. Not a single pistol-shot could be heard anywhere in the city. Then all at once, at 8 o'clock, this eerie peace was blown apart by the total, all-out inferno of the Russians' fire-power. The house lay directly on the path of the fleeing Germans; surrounded by the roar of heavy artillery, it quaked and rattled down to its foundations.

In a moment of sudden distress, Vali realized that Juliska, the sheepdog, had been left outside in her kennel. She'd always taken the pet in during air raids and heavy fighting, but this time it had slipped her mind somehow. She hoped Juliska would be safe in the garden.

They could sleep very little in the basement that night, so

appalling and relentless was the noise of this final, lethal stage of the Siege.

In the morning, when things seemed to have calmed down somewhat, Vali and the others came up from the basement to survey the scene. The house had survived well. And the cannon had disappeared from the back garden. But Juliska, the beautiful young Komondor from the lowlands, lay dead beside her kennel, her body riddled with bullets, her blood frozen on the snow.

It was never clear who had shot her. Many escaping Germans had tried to evade capture by hiding in gardens. It was all in vain. Three German soldiers lay dead on the snow in the garden of the house next door, and it was the same in many other gardens in the neighbourhood. Perhaps Germans intending to hide there had silenced the dog so that she couldn't give them away. Or perhaps the Russians had killed her because she interfered with the trap they had set for enemy soldiers. But whatever happened, the young dog's death saddened everyone in the house. Lajos said he would bury her at the end of the garden as soon as the ground had thawed out sufficiently. (He also helped the next-door neighbours bury the dead Germans in their garden.)

Although Juliska's death was very sad, the truth was that, once again, Vali and the others of the household were extremely lucky, because none of the German soldiers had attempted to seek refuge *inside* the house. Many of those desperate men had broken into private homes throughout that part of Buda and forced their occupants, usually at gunpoint, to shelter them. They hid in attics and cellars, hoping to avoid detection by the Russians. But in the days following the break-out the Russians scoured the entire area, entering each house and searching it from top to bottom, until they had tracked down virtually every hiding German soldier. When they were found, they were either shot or taken prisoner. The occupants of the house in which they took shelter, on the other hand, were invariably shot. Sometimes they hadn't even been aware of their hiding Germans. Several of Vali's neighbours met their deaths in this way.

107

When a group of Russian soldiers came to search 47d, they hammered loudly on the front door. Zsóka didn't open the door quickly enough for their liking, so they fired a round of ammunition through the French doors of the dining room, missing her by inches. Then they stormed in and turned the house upside down.

There were a few Germans who managed to escape detection for a longer period. Living outdoors on the run, they were forced to eat anything they could get hold of in order to stay alive in the freezing winter conditions. Their diet consisted mainly of mice and horseflesh.

Shortly after the Germans' capitulation, the Russians herded their captives out of Budapest, including the wounded men who'd been lying in the dressing station under the Castle. Thousands of POWs were marched up Budakeszi Avenue, as the main westward route out of the city. It was a gruesome sight, bearing a horrible similarity to the previous November's death marches to Hegyeshalom. Men barely able to walk were beaten and driven on mercilessly.

All of a sudden, in the middle of this procession which had been passing Vali's house for hours, there was heard the most horrifying howl of anguish imaginable. At first Vali couldn't tell whether the sound was human. She was in her bedroom at the time and immediately ran out on to the balcony.

The howl was repeated, and she saw that it came from one of the wounded captives, a young man with a bloody, bandaged leg. Unable to continue, he'd fallen by the roadside, and now a mounted Russian soldier was trying to drive him on. His nervous horse was trampling on the German, whose cries of pain were too much for Vali to bear.

Unable to control her rage and using the strongest Russian words she knew, she screamed at them to stop. Her voice rang out over the garden and was heard by Fyodor and Nadjuska in the room below. In an instant they had rushed upstairs, grabbed Vali and pulled her indoors.

They implored her never to do such a dangerous thing again. 'Don't you know they could shoot you for that?'

Ten

It was mid-February, shortly after the Siege was over, that Fyodor and Nadjuska received orders to move on to western Hungary, where the fighting was still in progress. Bidding Vali an affectionate farewell (Nadjuska cried shamelessly), they handed over their billet to a three-man Russian documentary film crew which had been recording the fall of Budapest for posterity (and propaganda). Now they were filming its aftermath: the guiding role of the victorious Red Army and the good comrades in establishing order once more.

The three young men, one of whom was Jewish, were good-natured and gregarious. Vali, after all the films she had made, was naturally at home with cameramen and technicians, and they all got on very well. They brought with them a great deal of equipment, which they kept in the sitting room, and each day they drove off in their car to whatever scene they'd been instructed to film.

No film-maker could have wished for more dramatic material. The sight of the capital after the Siege and the wretched state of its population made for the most riveting footage. The city was virtually one big bomb site. Opposite the burnt-out skeleton of the Castle the row of elegant, riverside hotels which had given Budapest so much of its international flavour lay in ruins. Almost all the windows of the city had been shattered. Bodies lay on the streets, intermingled with the blasted-out contents of buildings. And in the city zoo only fourteen animals out of 3,000 had survived. After Berlin and Warsaw, Budapest was the most devastated capital of the war. And with no infrastructure left, it was also one of the coldest and darkest.

Shops and warehouses had been looted by the Nazis, the Arrow Cross and the Red Army. Industry was severely disrupted as three-quarters of the city's factories were damaged. There was no longer an effective transportation system – many roads and over 2,000 bridges had been bombed, cars, lorries and the majority of trains (bulging with plunder) had been expropriated by the retreating Germans, making it impossible to transport food from the provinces to the capital. The only available meat for the city's starving inhabitants came from the dead horses on the streets. They were forced to sell their possessions in order to obtain what little food there was. Children continued to die of malnutrition. Throughout the countryside, fifty per cent of Hungary's livestock and thirty per cent of its agricultural machinery had been plundered. This was a disaster for a predominantly agricultural economy.

As if all these hardships and miseries were not enough, life was made very dangerous for the people of Budapest by their very 'liberators', the Red Army. In his report to Moscow, Malinovsky had grossly over-estimated the number of German and Hungarian POWs captured by the end of the Siege. He had put the number at 110,000 when the real figure was only half as many. It was too late to revise the estimate; it had been passed on to Stalin. Rather than incur his wrath by admitting to the error, Malinovsky supplied the missing thousands by rounding up innocent civilians on the streets of Budapest and dispatching them to prison camps in the Soviet Union. Fifty thousand were abducted in this way. Many never returned. Others came back only after several years' imprisonment.

The womenfolk weren't safe, either. By the tens of thousands they were raped in their dark cellars at night, often by soldiers who were drunk (a large percentage of these were Mongolians, perhaps Vali's heavy-breather among them). There was an abrupt and severe rise in the incidence of syphilis in the city. The Red Army was truly extraordinary: not only did the male soldiers rape women but there were several reports of female soldiers raping Hungarian men.

110

The army, quite simply, went on the rampage. They broke into and looted houses and apartments, often setting them on fire for no reason, and robbed people on the streets. There were military policemen about, trying to curb the excesses of their more crazed compatriots, but they were not too successful. So the long-suffering citizens of this crushed city were terrorized and tormented by the glorious heroes of the Red Army. That, however, was not recorded for posterity in the documentary films made by the crew quartered at 47d Budakeszi Avenue.

★

In the middle of February 1945, with the Siege just over, Vali was finally able to venture out in search of Paul Barabás. For nearly two months she'd been forced to stay at home and had lost contact with everyone. He would have been unable to reach her during the fighting, so there was no reason for Vali to suppose that, because she had not heard from him, he had come to harm.

The only means of transportation then was by *konflis* – private horse-drawn carriage. Vali was driven in one to her good friend Klári Tolnay's villa on Rose Hill, where Barabás had his *pied-à-terre*. When she arrived, she found the elegant house empty and badly damaged by bombs. Paul's rooms were in complete disarray. His books, papers and belongings were all over the floor, as if the place had been ransacked, and everything was covered with a layer of plaster dust. There was no indication that he had been there recently.

Klári herself, when she realized that her house was virtually on the Front Line as the Siege was about to begin, had retreated to the film studios in Buda, together with a large group of well-known film actors and directors. Barabás had not gone with her. Vali hoped that he and his family were somewhere safe. Surely he would be in touch with her soon.

And now, just in case she thought things might begin to ease up a bit, the house became suddenly full of refugees again.

One night Baroness Kóhner and her family appeared on the doorstep in great distress. The elderly, widowed Baroness (she was Christian but her husband had been a Jew) owned a grand

111

mansion further up Budakeszi Avenue. She told Vali what had happened.

On Christmas Eve, when the Soviets first entered Buda, her mansion was raided by soldiers who, with screams of abuse, smashed her windows, broke her furniture and generally pillaged her property. She, her pregnant daughter and her son-in-law were able to escape from the marauders through the assistance of two devoted servants.

Since then they had been hiding out wherever they could, fearing for their lives. The Baroness's daughter, nicknamed 'Baby', had given birth to her son in a cold, dirty cellar during the fiercest bombing of the Siege. And now they had nowhere to go. They were terrified of the Russians, especially Charlie, the Baroness's son-in-law, who'd heard that Hungarian men by the thousands were being dragged away as POWs. Would Vali take them in for a little while?

What a question. That night they slept in Vali's own bedroom – the Baroness, 'Baby' and her baby, and Charlie. Vali moved into the smaller room next door, happily unaware that the 'little while' would stretch to four months.

At almost the same time, Tessa appeared. She was the daughter of one of Vali's closest friends, the great classical actress Emilia Márkus, who also had a mansion nearby. Emilia, who was much older than Vali, was a vivacious, volatile, eccentric woman, capable of getting up to any amount of mischief in order to impose her will upon her family. She had two daughters: Tessa, the wife of a Swedish opera singer, and Romola, the wife of the brilliant but insane ballet dancer, Vaclav Nijinsky. Once, in order to prevent her grand-daughter from marrying somebody she disliked, Emilia demanded that Vali seduce the young fiancé at once and thus put an end to the whole business. She was furious when Vali rejected the idea.

Tessa, trapped in Hungary during the last year of the war, had been unable to join her husband in Sweden. Now, as she couldn't cross from Buda to Pest, she was separated from her mother, too. Emilia, one of the most prominent members of the National Theatre Company, had left her vulnerable house on Hidegkúti Avenue, near to Budakeszi Avenue, at the outset

112

of the Siege and opted for the sanctuary of the theatre's imposing building in Pest. Its dressing rooms had been turned into bedrooms for some of the members of the company. Their celebrity, and the prestige of the great National itself, afforded them a measure of protection from both the Nazis and the Soviets.

When Tessa arrived at the house of her mother's friend, she was desperate. Feverishly ill with cystitis, she was also cold and famished and had nothing but the clothes she was wearing. She'd been having a rough time during the Siege and had somehow lost contact with Emilia.

She moved in. There were no doctors available then, so the woman (who was a few years older than Vali) was simply put to bed and fed and given some aspirin and allowed to sleep.

Once more, the modest 'dacha' was peopled to the brim: there was Aunt Karolin and Uncle Lajos, Zsóka and her gold-toothed niece, the three-man Russian film crew, the Baroness and Baby and Charlie and their infant, the sick Tessa . . . and Vali Rácz, by now a very war-weary *chanteuse*. Thirteen in all. There were people sleeping in every room. There was still no running water – it had to be fetched in buckets from the municipal well. And how on earth was she to feed everyone? It was even more difficult to obtain food now than it had been some months earlier when the five Jews and the deserter had been hiding there. She longed for Sasha and his aides. They had so considerately brought her their spoils of war. It was different with the film crew; they were mere amateurs when it came to pillage.

★

By early March the situation began to improve. In the streets of Budapest the ice and snow were thawing; the approach of spring promised a much-needed relief from harsh weather, and people's spirits began to pick up a little, as they faced the colossal task of reconstructing their city. The Hungarians had always been a resilient lot.

Tessa recovered from her illness, and when she was well enough to cross the river on the pontoon bridge erected by the

Russians, Vali gathered together a bundle of clothes and some other necessary items for her. Tessa said she was only going to say goodbye to Emilia, because she intended to leave straight away for Sweden to rejoin her husband.

And then the film crew departed. They headed towards Berlin to capture on celluloid the Grand Finale – the defeat of the Third Reich and the destruction of its capital. They looked forward with excitement to the battle for Berlin. They left some of their equipment behind at Vali's house, telling her they would return for it when it was all over, on their way back to Russia.

They were the last of Vali's Russian 'guests'. Times were still difficult, even treacherous, in Budapest, but the war had moved on and most of the active fighting forces had moved with it. Billets were no longer required in such numbers. Vali dared to hope for a gradual return to a more normal existence. She was eager to re-establish contact with her parents in Gölle; there had been no communication between them since the fall of Transdanubia the previous December. The telephone lines were still not functioning. There were no telegraphic services. She wrote to them, but there was no way of telling whether her letters had arrived.

It was precisely at this moment, when the winter was about to make way for spring, and when, weakened and worn out by a seemingly endless series of tribulations, Vali at last began to feel a renewal of faith in the future, that she was forced to confront the spectre of her own death.

At first she felt no alarm – perhaps she should have heard the warning bell, but she wasn't worried because she believed that her innocence would protect her.

One afternoon in the middle of March a group of three men, describing themselves as members of a newly established local 'council', turned up at the house. They claimed to be making a routine house search. Vali, by now used to people of all kinds coming and going around her, let them in and watched casually as they opened cupboards and drawers and examined all the letters and documents they found in the roll-top desk in her bedroom.

114

And then one of the men came across her pocket diary of the previous year. Slowly he turned each page and read the daily entries. Towards the end of the diary he found something which obviously interested him. He showed it the others, who seemed equally intrigued. They exchanged meaningful glances. Then, a moment later, they put the diary down and abruptly took their leave.

After they had gone, Vali picked up the little book and leafed through it. What could it contain to interest them? It was full of now insignificant jottings. Then, on almost the last page, she saw something she had long forgotten about and the sudden sight of it gave her a nasty jolt. Clearly written in Paul Barabás's hand was the name 'Péter Hain', and beside it was the police chief's personal telephone number.

The following morning the men returned. This time, they told her, she would have to go with them to their headquarters.

'For what reason?'

'That will be explained when you get there.'

Still Vali felt no anxiety. Why should she? She had done nothing wrong.

'I don't know why these people can't just leave me alone,' she murmured to Karolin. 'Never mind, I'll be back soon.' She kissed her aunt goodbye.

Karolin gazed uneasily after her as she walked up the pathway to the gate, flanked by the strange men. It was all too reminiscent of that other occasion when she'd been taken away, the previous November. That time, too, she had expected to return home soon. But that had been on a cold, ominous day, a day permeated by that deathly, impenetrable fog which to her mind symbolized the whole Nazi nightmare that had engulfed their lives. That was all over now. They'd been liberated. And it was a calm, mild spring morning. Surely, this time everything would be all right.

The council's headquarters turned out to be in a disused school building in adjacent Labanc Street. Vali was taken to a room in which a dozen or so men and women were sitting in a semi-circle behind a table. She was made to sit on a chair facing them, on the other side of the table. The members of the council

115

regarded her with contempt.

Then one of them spoke. 'Valéria Rácz, you were a Nazi collaborator, weren't you?'

For a moment she was struck dumb by the shock of the accusation. 'How could you possibly say that?'

'We have evidence of it,' one of the women replied.

'What evidence?' Vali tried not to sound scornful, because she was now growing somewhat fearful of her mysterious accusers, and felt that she should defend herself with quiet dignity, not anger – that might only harm her case.

'That is none of your business!'

'Don't I have a right to know?'

The cold, callous answer which followed struck her like a blow from a fist. 'Collaborators have no rights.'

She looked desperately from one grim face to another, finding no comfort in any of them. One middle-aged man, though, was vaguely familiar to her. Where had she seen him before?

Feeling a little bolder, she asked, 'I demand my right to know what kind of council this is, and by what authority you have brought me here.'

'We are the new Communist committee for this district, made up of former partisans of a Jewish resistance movement. We know only too well, through our underground activities in this area, who the collaborators were.'

'Then you must know,' cried Vali, 'that during the Occupation I sheltered some of your fellow Jews in my house, at the risk of my own life! Does that sound like the act of a collaborator?'

'Where are these Jews? Are they prepared to speak for you?'

Crestfallen, Vali admitted that she had no idea where they were, or even if they were still alive. There was little hope of tracking them down in the total chaos of Budapest. But she explained to them that she must have been denounced by someone, and spoke about the raid by Hain's men and her arrest and interrogation at the Majestic.

'But you were released.'

'Yes, a friend was able to use his influence to get me out.'

116

'Which friend?'

'Paul Barabás, the writer and film director.'

There was an ominous silence in the room. 'We know all about Barabás,' a malevolent voice informed her. 'He worked for the Nazis in Berlin.'

'Yes, yes, but he wasn't a Nazi! On the contrary, he was involved in the resistance movement, the same as you. He wrote pamphlets . . .'

'Can that be proven? Where is he?'

'I don't know,' Vali whispered. 'I've had no word from him.' She felt numb.

'Wasn't your true role at the Majestic that of police informer?'

'No!'

'Péter Hain was not in the habit of releasing his prisoners.'

'There was no evidence against me,' she explained. 'They didn't find the Jews at my house.'

'Even so. You would have ended up like the others – on the road to Hegyeshalom. Why didn't you?'

She shook her head in dismay. 'I don't know . . .'

The committee of former partisans consulted quietly with each other for a moment, then one of them, the apparent 'chairman', turned to Vali. 'We shall consider your case. Go home now. You will be brought back here in twenty-four hours to hear our verdict.' His manner was very businesslike.

The woman who had spoken before raised an objection. 'I think we should put her downstairs in the cellar with the others. If she is allowed to go home, she might try to get away.'

But the chairman reassured her. 'Comrade, you've nothing to fear. She has nowhere to go.'

And someone else added, 'We will keep her under surveillance, naturally.'

Vali was led away. She walked home stunned, and when Karolin and Lajos questioned her, she told them what had happened in the school building as if describing a terrible and totally implausible dream. They, too, found it all hard to believe.

Lajos went to the school to reason with the members of the council. Surely he could make them see how misguided they

117

were regarding his niece. When he arrived and confronted them, he found to his surprise that he was well-acquainted with one of these ex-partisans. This boded well for his mission. But he met with no sympathy, and after a long, fruitless session, he went home in defeat. His word carried no weight; he was neither a Jew nor a Communist. The fact that, two decades earlier, he'd been hounded out of Count Bethlen's government because of his egalitarian tendencies was not enough for the comrades.

Vali was in a daze for the rest of the day, and that night as she lay in bed unable to sleep, she saw again the semi-circle of menacing faces before her. She concentrated on the one she thought she knew, trying to recall who the man was. Was he a neighbour? Were they acquainted?

Much later, exhausted by her efforts and on the brink of an uneasy sleep, she suddenly stiffened as she remembered exactly where she had seen that face before. He was the ranger in the nearby forest where she'd once gone for a walk with János, the young gardener's apprentice who had joined the Waffen-SS. János had showed her how to fire his rifle and at the sound of the shot the forest ranger had suddenly appeared out of nowhere. He had seen her, relaxed and playful, in the company of a Nazi soldier, a member of the dreaded 'death's head formation', and come to his own conclusion.

Would he believe her if she explained that she'd only wanted some fresh air and exercise after the ordeal of her internment? If she said that, as far as she was concerned, János was just the lad from Mr Kovács's nursery up the road who sometimes came to plant shrubs in her garden? János was later found dead in that forest. He'd gone back the next day to shoot a rabbit for her, but instead he was himself shot and killed by the Jewish partisans operating in the forest, perhaps by the friendly 'ranger' who'd chatted to them about the foxes and the deer.

She recollected something else which might not have escaped the attention of these local partisans: the visit of the two Wehrmacht officers, the admirers with whom she'd once dined at the Gellért. She had arranged it deliberately, so that her neighbours would not suspect her of harbouring Jews. She'd wanted that German jeep parked before her house; the more people to see it, the better. And how successful the ruse had been. The committee members would doubtless agree that no one with a house full of Jews was likely to invite Nazis over for a drink.

The picture was looking more and more dire. But still it all seemed like a bad dream, too fantastic to be true. And after all, what could they prove against her? Nothing. All their evidence was circumstantial. It occurred to her that perhaps they only wanted to give her a fright. To censure her. They were Jews enjoying their first taste of liberty for a long time. They were angry and vengeful, and with good reason. She could understand them. And somehow she would make them see how mistaken they were in her case.

They came for her again the next morning and wouldn't allow Karolin or anyone else to accompany her back to their headquarters. Once more she stood before the committee, the carefully arranged chairs, the rigid, merciless faces.

The chairman wasted no time. As soon as there was complete silence and all eyes were on Vali, he addressed her in a solemn voice. 'Valéria Rácz, we have found you guilty. The punishment for your offence is death. This sentence is to be carried out tomorrow morning at ten o'clock, when you will be taken from your home and shot. You are allowed to go home now to prepare for your death.'

She felt the panic surging through her. 'You can't! It isn't possible! I have not committed any crime!'

'Your sentence has been passed.'

'This isn't a proper court. I demand to be heard in a legitimate court of the National Hungarian Government. They must judge whether I am guilty or innocent.'

'There is no necessity for that. It has already been decided: tomorrow morning you will be taken out and shot into a lime-pit.' The chairman stood up. 'And now you may leave.' With that she was dismissed, and escorted back home.

Karolin was beside herself with grief. She wept uncontrollably, her arms around Vali, who sat limply on her bed. The others in the house, Lajos, the Baroness and Baby and Charlie,

Zsóka and Marika, all came in to see what the matter was. They stared in shock and disbelief when Karolin, through her sobs, told them the verdict of the committee.

The past year had taken a heavy toll on Vali's constitution. She was pallid and thin, never having regained the weight she lost during her incarceration. Her nerves were ruined from lack of sleep, worry and the relentless strain of war. The old spirit was gone. In her weak and despondent state, she hadn't sufficient will or stamina to fight on. It seemed easier simply to give in.

In a thin, tired voice, she asked Karolin to fetch the Jesuit priest who had come to ask for help during the Siege when his church was being abused by Russian soldiers. Now he could return the favour: she wanted him to administer the last rites.

Her strongest emotion just then was sorrow for her parents. She would never see them again, and as she had no siblings, she would be rendering them childless.

Karolin managed to compose herself enough to go to the church, and she returned with the priest a little later. In the meanwhile, word of Vali's plight spread throughout the neighbourhood, and one by one people began to arrive to pay their last respects to the *chanteuse*. In the end there were nearly a dozen tearful neighbours up in her bedroom.

The Jesuit's manner was gentle and soothing. He drew the curtains, lit some incense and began the rites. Vali kneeled down on the floor in the middle of the room, her palms together and her eyes closed, while the priest stood over her, his hand resting on her head. The others, too, kneeled down around them and watched mournfully, some praying, some trying to stifle their weeping. The housekeeper was intrigued by the spectacle, but doubtless more concerned about losing her job than that Vali's soul should end up in the right place.

The priest intoned his words of Latin as the smell of burning incense slowly filled the dusky room. Vali surrendered herself, feeling already within reach of some other world, where there was serenity at last. After her brief, whispered confession, the priest prepared to administer Holy Communion by placing the wafer on her tongue.

At the very moment that she parted her lips, heavy boots were heard thundering up the stairs.

The door burst open and a familiar voice demanded loudly in Russian, 'Chto takoe – what's all this?'

Vali opened her eyes. It was Sasha, wearing his customary black leather coat. A bandage was visible beneath his officer's cap; he'd received a head wound in the Balkans. Behind him stood his two aides.

He strode across the room, brushed the priest aside and pulled Vali up off her knees. 'Chto takoe?' he repeated, holding her by the arms.

She was dizzy and bewildered, as if she'd been aroused from a stupor. In faltering Russian she told him that she was going to be shot the following day. She'd been sentenced by the Communists.

'What have you done?' he asked.

'Nothing.'

'Did you kill someone?'

'No.'

'Committed some other crime?'

'No.'

He held her more tightly. 'You have to tell me the truth – do you understand? Because if you're guilty, there is nothing I can do for you.'

'I'm innocent . . .'

'Then I believe you. Put on your coat and take me to these Communists now!'

Before the open-mouthed stares of the assembled company, he led her out of the room, down the stairs and outside to his jeep. He sat her in the back in between his aides, jumped into the front beside his driver, and they roared off around the corner to Labanc Street and the disused school.

The committee was still there in the same room, conducting its affairs. When Sasha burst into their midst with Vali in tow, they looked up, startled and speechless. From the expressions on their faces it was immediately apparent with what awe they regarded this high-ranking officer of the Red Army.

Sasha addressed them forcefully in rapid Russian, and Vali

121

understood that he forbade the council to take any further action in her case until he had himself consulted with higher Soviet military authorities. Then he took her out of the room and told her to sit down in a chair in the hallway and wait.

He left for the headquarters of the nearest military unit in order to contact the central Soviet command post in Pest. He had to rely solely on the military radio transmitter, an often slow and cumbersome procedure. It took half an hour to make the connection.

Urgently he sought to verify Vali's credentials as an anti-fascist and to obtain the authority to rescue her from the clutches of the bloodthirsty committee. He knew that he was powerless to intervene independently in a matter over which he had no jurisdiction. He was passed from one official to another on the crackling line.

He referred to the member of the Communist resistance who had sought his help two months earlier at Vali's house. Sasha had arranged for him to cross the river in order to rejoin his comrades in Pest. The man had vouched for her total political acceptability. Sasha remembered his name and tried to have him traced. His testimony would surely carry weight with the committee.

In the end, it proved unnecessary. Vali had already passed through the routine interrogation process with several Soviet military officials on the Pest side. Some of them had already been convinced of her innocence before they saw her; they simply wanted to meet the film star and ask her out on a date. Before long Sasha was given full authority to order Vali's unconditional release.

Vali sat in the hallway for two hours. When at last Sasha came back, he took her by the hand and together they entered the room where the committee had been awaiting the outcome of the colonel's inquiries.

'Now,' he declared, making his intense displeasure quite clear to the suddenly tame-looking group, 'this woman has been completely exonerated. She is coming with me. And she is not to be bothered by any of you again!'

The chairman began to speak, but Sasha didn't stop to hear it.

Still holding her by the hand, he led her out to the waiting jeep, put her once again in between his ever-present aides, and they all drove back to 47d Budakeszi Avenue.

Karolin flung her arms around Sasha's neck and wept with relief. He happily accepted the invitation to stay for lunch. And that was when Vali and the others learnt that Sasha was only passing through Budapest that day on his return from Rumania. That same evening he and his troops would have to continue westward to the combat zone. For Vali, his chance arrival in the city on that particular day had been nothing less than a miracle.

Later, when they were alone, Sasha told her about his time in the Balkans. He was frank with her, confessing that he had had an affair with a Rumanian woman in Bucharest – an actress. (He seemed to have developed a taste for them.) But that had only been a fling, nothing important, he said. Nothing like his passionate feelings for her.

When they parted that evening, he promised Vali that he would come back to Budapest once more. The war would be over soon. And he couldn't go home without saying goodbye.

Eleven

Early one morning while still in bed Vali heard raised voices downstairs. She quickly put on her dressing gown and went down to see what was happening.

She found Charlie in the front hall being dragged towards the door by two Russian soldiers, looking frightened and protesting ardently. His young wife, Baby, was standing by in obvious distress, her infant in her arms. It seemed that her worst fears had come true.

'*Chte takoe?*' demanded Vali.

'He's a German – a soldier trying to escape!' replied one of the Russians. 'He must come with us!'

'It isn't true!' wailed Baby. Her son was starting to cry, upset by all the shouting.

Karolin was there, too, tearfully pleading with the Russians in her soft, plaintive manner. It was having no effect. The Baroness now came downstairs and gasped when she saw her son-in-law being roughly handled by two strange men.

Vali meanwhile reasoned with the would-be abductors. 'Of course he isn't German. He is a Hungarian. Look – this is his wife and child, this woman here is his mother-in-law – can't you see? He is living here with his family.' She became suddenly impassioned. 'I am telling you the truth. *Chestnoe slovo* – I swear it!'

The men loosened their grip on Charlie. They exchanged looks with each other, then gazed for a minute or two at the little family group, at the young wife clutching her crying baby and the trembling elderly lady. Vali could see them hesitating.

They let go of Charlie. 'All is in order, then,' said one of the Russians with a curt nod to Vali. And they turned around and left.

It was early spring. The household was, happily, now without two of its former occupants: Marika, the blonde wench who had so relished being liberated by the 'Ivans' (as the Hungarians called them), and her Aunt Zsóka.

Marika made her way back to her uncle's house in Pest, hoping to be received back into the bosom of her Arrow Cross family. Her uncle, of course, was still in the Reich, but it would not be long before he was brought back to face charges as a war criminal.

Soon afterwards, Zsóka was sacked. Vali had had enough of her shifty ways. And the woman hadn't even thanked her, after the Nazi Occupation was finally over, for risking her own life to shelter her deserter son. (The son never returned to express his gratitude, either.) Vali didn't bother to replace her because, with ever-helpful Karolin living at the house, she had no need of a housekeeper.

Some days after Zsóka left, Vali found that the disgruntled employee had retaliated against her dismissal. A pigskin case containing all the fine cosmetics and make-up she had brought back from Berlin in 1943, and which she had been saving for her eventual return to work, had disappeared from its place in the basement. She was distressed by the loss. In the war-ravaged Europe of 1945 items such as those were not only worth a fortune, they were virtually impossible to replace. They had also been a memento of Paul Barabás, for it was he who had taken her shopping for those things on that last day in Berlin, before she caught the train home.

As the days passed without word from Barabás, Vali grew ever more pessimistic about his fate. She knew that if he were still alive and in Budapest, he would have been to see her, or contacted her somehow. She wanted desperately to find out what had happened to him, but there was still no way of reaching mutual friends who might have information. So many people had been displaced, scattered by the Siege, bombed out or had simply disappeared. There was confusion in the capital. Vali had never met Barabás's wife, and she was not eager to seek her out now. So she waited.

One day she received an unexpected visit from Károly Barabás and an unfamiliar woman whom, at first, she took to be his mother. Vali hoped for some news, but was dismayed when Károly merely asked her whether she knew anything of his father's whereabouts. And that was when Vali finally understood how black the picture was.

On the morning of 24 December 1944, while Károly delivered Vali's present, Paul was making his way to Rose Hill to fetch some papers and manuscripts from his flat while there was still (as he perceived it) time to do so. He planned to work on them over the next few weeks at the house of his friend, Szabolcs Fényes, where he and his family were then staying. Fényes was a popular composer who knew Vali well; she had performed many of his songs. His house was in Eagle Hill – a safer part of Buda, as it was out of the immediate battle zone.

Paul was not alone. The caretaker of the Fényes house had accompanied him, in order to help carry the papers back. After agreeing to meet Károly at a specific time at the bottom of the hill, near the beginning of Budakeszi Avenue, the two men headed towards the Tolnay villa. They heard the sound of distant gunshots. Not far away from them, armoured vehicles were rumbling through the empty residential streets of Buda. Advance patrols had been sent in for reconnaissance. The coming Siege hung in the air, menacing and inescapable.

Károly left Vali's house promptly and hastened to the agreed meeting place. He waited for his father and the caretaker to arrive. He stood there for over two hours, but they never came. In the end, not daring to wait any longer, he made his way back to the Fényes house alone. Since that morning, no one had seen or heard from either Paul Barabás or the caretaker.

The woman with Károly was the caretaker's wife. She had tried everything she could to find out what had become of her husband, but to no avail. She now revealed something which filled Vali with dread. Barabás, the caretaker's wife told her, had left the Fényes house that morning with two different identity documents on his person, in case he was challenged by the authorities – one was designed to be shown to the Germans, the other to be offered to the Russians for inspection. Some of the details in them varied, to make him acceptable to either side. But Vali had already heard what happened to those who were caught at this game: they were shot without further ado as 'spies'. No questions asked.

So it seemed unlikely that the two men had been captured by the Russians and sent as POWs to the Soviet Union. Vali and the wives of the caretaker and Barabás were forced to assume, in the end, that their bodies had ended up in one of the mass graves dug for the city's numerous anonymous dead. The circumstances of their disappearance would forever remain shadowy and inconclusive.

Vali grieved for her old confidant and mentor, the man who had perhaps loved her best of all. It was a terrible irony that he had managed against the odds to save her from the fate of the others at the Majestic, and yet not been able to save himself. He had been careless, the way he was careless about writing Hain's name into her diary. Why didn't he stay put, why did he have to venture out into the treacherous streets? But she could not blame him for anything now. She missed him profoundly.

★

The poster read:

The Hungarian Democratic Youth Alliance
XII District Branch
is organizing a
GALA PERFORMANCE
on Saturday, 14 April 1945, at 3 o'clock
at the Theatre of Buda
in the Cistercian Gymnasium, 27 Szent Imre Herceg Street

Underneath, in two columns, were the names of the performers taking part in the event. Vali Rácz was one of them. It was her first public appearance since her engagement at the Vidám Theatre in *Romeo and Piroska* had been curtailed by her sojourn at the Hotel Majestic.

The 14 April was ten days after the whole of Hungary was declared 'liberated', and the war was over at last for the Magyar people. A new era was to begin, and the very words 'democratic' and 'youth', so proudly displayed on that poster, boded well for it.

On 13 April the Provisional Hungarian Government established in Debrecen the previous December moved to Budapest. Its National Assembly comprised 230 deputies from a surprisingly wide political spectrum: there were seventy-two Communists, fifty-seven from the Smallholders' Party, thirty-five Social Democrats, nineteen trade union representatives and twelve members of the National Peasant Party; the remainder were either independent or from marginal parties.

By the time the Provisional Government reached the capital, the Russians, the Communists and various Communist-run organizations were already installed in the best public buildings. Because of the devastation there was a dire shortage of usable premises. The Government was therefore allocated only shabby and damaged tenements. But even so, the politicians of the newly revived parties were optimistic about the future as they set to the task of rebuilding the country.

It was, to all outward appearances, the birth of a genuine coalition. The Communists, even the Muscovites newly arrived in Hungary with the Red Army, seemed most amenable to the idea of power-sharing and rule by the majority. At the very first session of the Assembly, Ernő Gerő, one of the leading Muscovites, claimed that the policy of the Hungarian Communist Party was a 'Hungarian, democratic and national policy'. And the politicians of the coalition parties took him at his word. After all, under Nazi domination they had struggled side by side in the underground movement with the Communists to defeat their common enemy, and a certain spirit of brotherhood had developed between them.

In the new Cabinet, the Communists, Social Democrats and Smallholders had two portfolios each, the Peasant Party had one. The Cabinet also included five non-affiliated members, and even an aristocrat: Count Géza Teleki, son of the one-time prime minister Paul Teleki who had killed himself in 1941 in

128

protest against Hungary's forced invasion of Yugoslavia. Prime Minister Béla Miklós and two other ministers had been generals in the Horthy regime.

So the political set-up seemed most promising. But behind the scenes things were completely different. While on the surface power was being divided between the parties, the true reins of power were held by the Communists, who were sponsored not only by the controlling Soviet military forces, but even more insidiously, by the MVD – the Soviet secret police. Under the auspices of the MVD the most comprehensive, subversive and lethal power base ever known in Hungary had already been put into effect. The ÁVO, the secret, Moscow-led police force which was the inner core of the Hungarian Communist Party, the 'party within a party', would over the coming years make the Gestapo men seem quite amateurish by comparison.

In 1849 the Magyar poet József Bajza wrote, 'Liberty without democracy is as inconceivable as illumination without a source of light.' His words were to have a tragic echo across the century. For in 1945, behind the façade of democracy, the reality was this: the key government positions were securely in Communist hands, and the Communists retained effective control even when apparent authority was given to non-Communists. 'Fellow travellers' often provided a useful front for the promotion of Communist policy. No government officials could be appointed without Russian approval.

From the beginning the Communists endeavoured to penetrate and seize control of the trade union movement, one of their essential tools. Through the unions they could then easily infiltrate every type of workplace. To initiate this process, as early as 23 February, the workers of the capital had been addressed by Mátyás Rákosi, the Party's general secretary.

Rákosi was not only a Muscovite. This close friend of both Lenin and Stalin was one of the original Bolsheviks. He had spent sixteen years in Hungarian prisons as an illegal Communist and for his part in the 1919 Béla Kun revolution (he was one of the numerous Jews involved in the brief but tyrannical Communist regime which had so greatly contributed to the rise of anti-Semitic feelings in the 1920s). He was released from prison and went to the Soviet Union in 1940 during the period of the Nazi-Soviet peace pact. Now he had returned with a vengeance.

(It is interesting to note that Rákosi's 'socialist' tendencies were first awakened during his brief spell in England before the First World War. While he was living in London and working in a bank, he sought out the British Labour Party. Even after he became a merciless dictator, this pudgy little bald man preserved the appearance of a bank clerk.)

The Communists despised genuinely left-wing politicians, whose convictions and independence of mind were anathema to an organization which sought total control above all else, with social reforms as a mere by-product. Many ex-Nazis, on the other hand, were welcomed into the Party. The Communists knew only too well that these adherents to dictatorship could switch their allegiance instantly from Hitler to Stalin.

The truth was that the non-Communist parties were in many ways as progressive as the Communists claimed to be. They realized that change was long overdue in economic and social matters and wasted no time in ushering in reforms. Already on 15 March, while still in Debrecen, the Provisional Government had issued the Land Reform Bill. This brought down the curtain on the old semi-feudal system of land ownership in Hungary whereby fifty per cent of the country's arable land was owned by only 2,000 landowners. This land was now taken away and distributed amongst 642,000 peasants. (Of almost equal importance, the reforms took away the vast lands owned by the Church. With no economic base left, it was a bankrupt and powerless institution.)

The former landowners – mainly from the aristocracy and the gentry – suddenly became the *nouveaux pauvres*. The magnificent Park Club on Stefánia Avenue, the aristocrats' exclusive hang-out, was turned into a club for the officers of the Allied Control Commission. And here in 1945 the impoverished counts and barons would come, no longer as members, but as grateful guests of the new 'nobility' – the American army officers. With their dollars the most sought-after currency in Europe, they

130

really did live like aristocrats. They rented beautiful villas, hired servants, wined and dined in regal style.

The ex-landowners, on the other hand, now owned practically nothing at all. In order to survive, for the first time in their lives they had to find regular employment. They became cab drivers and cleaners. What they could salvage of their wealth – a watch, a piece of jewellery, a silver cigarette case – they tried to sell surreptitiously to officers at the Park Club, generally using the bartenders and waiters as go-betweens. It was mainly the Americans who patronized the club, plus a few British officers. The Russians on the whole, stayed away. They were paid in pengős, and could not afford this lavish lifestyle.

For a long time after the close of hostilities, Hungary was kept isolated from the West by the ACC. It was dominated by the Russians, who often ignored the wishes of the American and British members. Diplomatic contacts with other countries could not be renewed without its permission, and permission was often withheld. The chairman of the ACC in Hungary was Marshal Kliment Voroshilov, a leading Bolshevik and People's Commissar for Defence. It was he who, together with Marshal Zhukov, had successfully repelled the German attack against Leningrad in 1943. At the end of the Siege of Budapest, Voroshilov not only took over the city from the defeated Nazi commandant, but, it was rumoured, he took over the commandant's mistress as well.

★

At long last the war in Europe reached its end. The great Hungarian novelist and playwright, Sándor Márai, wrote in his diary:

> These are the headlines on the newspapers' front pages: Berlin has fallen, Hitler is dead, the Allies have marched into Hamburg. No one pays attention to the news; I don't, either. Hardly anyone buys the papers. A year ago, what we would have given to read news like this in the papers! Now it's a matter of indifference what happens to Hitler and Germany. Lard is important, and bacon, and bread. The rest one hears

131

about and waves aside.

No one has a salary, and if they do, they can only buy a kilo of bread and a few kilos of lard with it. So who can afford the 2,000-pengő geese and the 3,000-pengő hams hanging in the shop windows?

Towards the end of May, when a beautiful, warm spring had finally descended upon the rubble-strewn capital, Vali found herself back in business again. She received a three-month engagement at the Café de la Paix in Freedom Square, on the Pest side. She was to be the first post-war nightly entertainer at the large, popular establishment.

The American Embassy was also situated in this square, and the Yanks (the most favoured of the Allied victors) soon formed the regular clientele of the Café de la Paix. As they paid in dollars, the management was able to give Vali her salary in dollars. This was an inestimable advantage, because by this time a hyper-inflation of unprecedented proportions was beginning to take its grip on the country.

Before the war a dollar was worth about five pengős. By December of 1945, it was worth 275,000 pengős. Inflation began to rise drastically during the summer and autumn after the war, and eventually the pengő was being counted in units of millions, then billions, trillions and quadrillions. The day after a person received his weekly wage, it wouldn't even cover the cost of his bus ticket to work. In the end a world record was achieved: money was printed in figures bearing no less than eighteen zeros. (This desperate situation continued until August 1946, when the currency was finally stabilized by the introduction of the forint.)

One dollar was considered a small fortune. The other highly desirable form of currency was the so-called 'Napoleon', a French gold coin dating from Napoleonic times, which was then worth about $18. They began to turn up here and there, quite mysteriously, and they were favoured because they were small and easy to hide on one's person. It was illegal to be paid in or to possess either of these, so each week Vali stashed most of her dollars away in an old rabbit hutch in the garden.

Inevitably, a thriving black market came into being. This took various forms. One practice was to go to the countryside, purchase a large amount of food, then smuggle it across the border to Austria (where starvation was more widespread) and exchange the food for items impossible to get in Hungary – e.g. nylon stockings, soap, whisky and cigarettes – which the Austrians had managed to acquire from the occupying American forces. These luxuries could then be sold on the streets of Budapest for the coveted dollars.

Lieutenant Simon Bourgin was an American reporter on his first visit to Central Europe in October 1945. In an article for *Life* Magazine he wrote,

> Ten minutes after I arrived in Budapest I was offered two cameras, a Rolleiflex and a Leica, and two German pistols for American dollars. The would-be vendors were the head-waiter and a doorman at Budapest's swankiest eating place. The rest of the day I was approached at least a dozen times by Hungarians who had silks, gems, watches and cameras to sell for American dollars.
>
> The American dollar is king in Budapest today. The dollar here can buy anything – all the luxuries and fineries that the rest of Europe only dreams about. Mink coats, silk stockings and handmade boots are available in shops – for dollars. Steak, champagne and *crêpes suzette* are everyday fare in the restaurants and nightclubs. But only Americans and a few hundred newly rich Hungarians can afford them. [Those newly rich Hungarians were, of course, the profiteers, shady or otherwise.]

Bourgin was one of the many Americans frequenting the capital's nightspots, including the ones where Vali Rácz sang. But unlike most of his compatriots, he later became acquainted with her, and they were to develop a life-long friendship.

Vali was happy to be singing regularly again, and to be out at last from the house which had become almost like a prison during those cold and tragic winter months. But getting to and from the café each evening presented a considerable problem.

The only way to cross the river was by an assortment of ferries, for which people would have to queue for hours, or on the pontoon bridge. The only reliable means of transportation available to Vali was the bicycle which Nadjuska had fortunately managed to retrieve from the Russian thief. And with a limited electricity supply in the city, the streets were dark at night, especially in Buda.

So, each night after her performance, she would have to cycle back all the way from Freedom Square to Budakeszi Avenue, about five miles away. The last part of the journey, once she had left livelier, commercial Pest and entered the lonely residential streets of Buda, was petrifying. It would have been unpleasant and somewhat risky even under normal circumstances, but this was at a time when people were still being killed or robbed and women were still being raped by the often-drunk Russian soldiers who swarmed through the capital. (Simon Bourgin recalled forty-four years later: 'If you were an American, beautiful ladies might come to your table as the restaurant closed and beg to be escorted to their homes – respectable ladies as well as tarts – as there was shooting every night in the streets.')

József, her erstwhile friend and doctor, who had driven her home from the theatre so often the previous autumn, was without his Red Cross ambulance and no longer able to oblige. Vali saw less of him after the war. He realized that, although she had needed him, she had never been in love with him. After a while he became interested in another woman and it was with a certain relief that Vali made way for her.

When Vali was able to get her first short break from singing, she took the opportunity to visit her parents. The young friend who'd driven her out to a Swabian village to buy food shortly before the Siege began was able, by some miracle, to acquire the use of a private car. He now offered his services once more. So they set off for the Dunántúl.

After a long, dusty journey, they arrived unannounced at the L-shaped house in Gölle. There was an emotional reunion. Then the Ráczes expressed their annoyance that she hadn't come sooner.

'How could I have got here? By climbing on top of a train?'

There were few trains then, and they ran irregularly. The trains from Budapest were all besieged by people anxious to get out to the countryside to exchange clothes, shoes and other belongings for food from the peasants. So crowded were these trains that people were forced to sit even on the carriage roofs. Somehow, that wasn't Vali's style.

The Ráczes knew nothing of what had happened to their daughter over the past ten months since she left their house with Ilona, the young Jewess she took back to Budapest as her 'secretary'. They didn't know about her arrest and interrogation by Hain's men, or about the full fury of the prolonged Siege, or about the council of ex-partisans who were so eager to shoot her as a collaborator. They had received none of her letters.

They did, however, know about the dire food shortage in Budapest and had arranged for an acquaintance who was leaving for the capital to take with him a huge smoked ham for Vali. To thank him for his trouble, they presented him with a huge smoked ham as well. But he never got to Vali's house. He just kept both hams for himself and didn't show his face again.

Twelve

One day in June the Russian film crew returned, as they'd said they would, to pick up the equipment left behind at Vali's house. But there were only two of them now. Some time during the final days of the war one of the young men, the Jew, was hit by a stray bullet and died instantly.

They spent one night at the house, telling Vali and the others about the Red Army's final push to Berlin, and the capitulation of the ruined city. The following morning they prepared for their departure. They were going back home, realizing that they would probably never again be able to leave Stalin's Russia.

Slowly, reluctantly, they packed up all their things. Vali watched as they filled up several large film cans with sugar, taped them down and labelled them 'undeveloped film – not to be opened'. They knew only too well what they were going home to.

*

It was a balmy summer's evening. Vali was singing at the Café de la Paix. The place, as usual, was full of Americans, with a generous sprinkling of British military and diplomatic personnel. Vali had got to know several of them over the past weeks. They were fascinated by the glamorous Magyar with the seductive voice. She provided a rare pleasure in the dusty ruins of Budapest.

She was in the middle of one of her favourite old *chansons*, the musicians playing sweetly behind her, when she spotted a woman standing at the back of the room, watching her performance. They looked into each other's eyes, and the sudden shock of recognition made Vali miss the next few words of the song.

It was Vera Somló, the young Jewess with whom she had been imprisoned at the Majestic. It was almost inconceivable: she was still alive.

Vali smiled at her and when she continued the song her voice was trembling slightly. Automatically, she put her hand up to her neck and felt the gold chain with the heart-shaped pendant which Vera had given her for safe-keeping on the day they parted. By sheer coincidence, Vali had put it on earlier that evening.

Vera was smiling too, with tears in her eyes. She began to walk towards Vali, winding her way through the white-clothed tables. When the song was over the two women embraced. Vali removed the necklace and pressed it into Vera's hand.

'You see,' she whispered, 'I've looked after it for you.'

The story of Vera's escape from death was miraculous. On 8 December, two days after Vali was released on the whim of Péter Hain, Arrow Cross henchmen under the command of the sadistic young Catholic priest, Father András Kun, came to empty the Majestic of its remaining prisoners. Vera and her mother were among the large group of Jews made to march down from Swabian Hill to the District II Arrow Cross headquarters in Városmajor Street, run by Father Kun.

The place was an indescribable hell for any Jews who were brought there. Kun, who wore a pistol in the belt of his priest's frock, generally tortured his captives before dispensing with them. Vera saw a young girl being suffocated with her own blood-stained sanitary napkin and a man who had had his penis nailed to a table before being killed.

Kun ordered Vera to stand before him and strip naked. When she had done so, she observed that he was sexually roused by the sight.

'You call yourself a priest?' she cried out with disgust. 'You should be ashamed!' She spat into his face.

For this she was set upon by several of his men and beaten nearly to death, with her horror-struck mother looking on. Her skull was fractured, her jaw dislocated and the kicks she received (one of which hurled her literally into the air) caused a haemorrhage in her stomach. But the ordeal had only just begun.

She was dragged to her feet and told to get dressed and join the other prisoners. It was obvious that they were all going to be taken somewhere. She overheard one of the Arrow Cross men saying they had orders to send fifty Jews west to the border to work for the Reich. Despite the excruciating pain which filled every part of her body, Vera was able to count the number of prisoners in their group: sixty. What would they do with the surplus?

They began another march. Crossing into Pest at Margaret Island, they were taken down to the lower embankment before Parliament. Vera, supported by her mother, walked with great difficulty and was slowing down by this time. The group marched in a column, four-abreast, along the water's edge. That was when they heard the first shots.

Vera turned around and saw that, every few yards, two guards would pull someone out from the end of the column. Then one of the guards would shoot the person in the nape of the neck, while the other pushed him into the river. So, she told herself, this is how they will get rid of the ten extra prisoners.

The shooting went on for several minutes, the column becoming gradually shorter. Soon Vera noticed that she and her mother were almost at the end themselves. And then, a moment later, she turned around and saw that they were the next in line.

Suddenly her hair was yanked fiercely from behind. 'Come here, you with the frizzy hair!' a guard shouted.

'My hair isn't frizzy!' Vera shouted back, but her words were distorted because of her dislocated jaw. Once again she was not frightened but furious and she spat at her tormentor. It was mainly blood which came out of her mouth.

She felt the cold butt of a gun pressed against her neck, Then she heard shouts from a short distance away. Apparently

138

another guard, who'd been walking further up the column, decided to do a head-count and discovered that his zealous colleagues had already killed twenty-seven people, and they no longer had the required number of slave labourers. Indignantly, he told them to stop the shooting at once.

And so Vera was taken with the rest of the group to a building in Teleki Square, on Rákóczi Avenue, where they were to spend the night. Their train journey to an Austrian labour camp was scheduled for the following morning.

But one of the guards on duty in the prisoners' room, an elderly man who belonged to the right-wing Hungarista Party, turned out to be a family acquaintance of the Somlós, and he recognized the two women. Shocked by Vera's injuries, he cried, 'My God, what have they done to you?' Early the next morning he smuggled Vera and her mother out of the building and took them to the hospital in the Jewish ghetto, which was bordered on the south by Rákóczi Avenue.

Vera's injuries were treated in the hospital, and the next day she telephoned her sister, who was still living in Budapest with false papers and was in touch with Raoul Wallenberg. Her sister had new identity documents prepared at once for Vera and brought to her in the ghetto. Vera's red hair was dyed black and she was given new clothes. Concealing her wounds as best as she could, she was smuggled out through one of the ghetto gates.

She lived with her false identity until the liberation of Pest. Her parents survived, too – her mother in the ghetto, and her father, the 'retired colonel', on Rose Hill.

In 1946 Vera Somló again confronted Father Kun, who had been brought back from Germany by the Americans. On this occasion she was Crown witness for the prosecution at his trial as a war criminal. Largely on the basis of her testimony, he was sentenced to death and hanged.

Four decades later, recalling all that had happened to her during that winter of 1944–5, Vera Somló had this to say: 'They never frightened me, those Arrow Cross murderers. I wasn't the type they could intimidate. And I never once doubted, not even when I stood at the edge of the Danube with a gun at my neck, that I would live through it. I had to survive; it was my fate.'

★

That summer Vali learned that the five Jews she had hidden during the Nazi Occupation – Szerén and Jenő Mandel, Szerén's sister Ilona, and Margit Herzog and her daughter Marietta – had all survived the War.

When it became a little easier to get around the city, they called on her at the house to recount their stories. And Vali found out how she had been (accidentally) betrayed to the police in the first place. It was due to one careless mistake by Margit's husband, Dezső.

Late in November, Desző Keleti, still operating under the Christian identity of 'József Papp', planned an escape from Budapest to a part of Hungary already occupied by the Russians, where he felt he would be safe. He spoke fluent Russian and was eager to make contact with the liberation forces. He was good friends with a Hungarian pilot, and the two men devised a scheme together. Dezső would disguise himself in the uniform of a gendarme and the pilot would fly him out of the capital to Russian-held territory not far away.

It was a risky undertaking, which appealed to Dezső's sense of adventure. He now decided that, because something might go wrong during this escapade, he had better first write his will. He gave the will to his pilot friend, together with a letter containing information on where to find his wife and children in case he had to inform them of his death or capture. Margit and Marietta, he wrote, were 'staying with Vali, the *művésznő*' (an expression which means 'lady artist'). He then disclosed the address of the couple who had taken in their son, Péter.

Something did go terribly wrong, even before their attempted flight. The pilot came under the suspicion of the police because of an entirely different matter. His flat was searched, and Dezső's will and letter were found.

Péter and those harbouring him were arrested at once. As for the reference to the *művésznő*, they didn't have to think hard before adding the name 'Rácz' to Vali. Hence that black

140

morning of Sunday, 26 November, when they raided 47d. They had come to the house expecting to find Margit and Marietta. They left with only Vali. How they would have fumed had they learned that hidden in the house were not only the two people they were seeking, but another three Jews, and an army deserter, to boot.

Dezső was captured shortly before Christmas. Still masquerading as a gendarme, complete with plumed helmet, he was carousing one evening in a coffee house. His conspicuous behaviour made him suspect. He was interrogated, and when his lodgings were ransacked, forged documents were found. He was taken down to the Danube embankment, shot dead and thrown into the water. The liberation of Pest was less than a month away.

His tragedy was that, but for his recklessness, he would probably have survived. This flaw in his nature very nearly ended several other lives, as well.

When Marietta, in a blind panic after her close brush with Hain's men, disappeared into the cold fog that Sunday, she headed for the address which she most associated with comfort and support – 106 Andrássy Avenue, the Herzog family mansion. She knew that no members of her family would be there, but thought that perhaps the staff could shelter her.

She arrived at the magnificent residence and the front door was opened to her by the housekeeper, who gasped in horror at the sight of the anxious teenager.

'Get away at once, do you hear?' the woman urged her. 'The Nazis have occupied this house and they are down in the basement right now, studying their maps!'

Marietta fled down Andrássy Avenue, past the mansions and the 'House of Loyalty' – national headquarters of the Arrow Cross government. She thought of her uncle, the famous 'One-armed Imre' whose First World War decorations had protected him from Nazi persecution. He had a flat in another part of Pest – perhaps she could stay there? This gave her new hope.

Afraid that at any moment she might be stopped and questioned, she hurried through the gloomy streets. But when she reached Imre's flat, he wasn't there. She sat down on the staircase to wait. The porter passed by a little later and was shocked to find her.

'You must leave at once!' he whispered. 'Your uncle is gone – no one knows where he is now.'

Times had changed. When the Arrow Cross seized power a month earlier, even Imre was forced into hiding. One of the first acts of the Szálasi government was to revoke all exemptions for Jews, even for war heroes. Marietta didn't know where to begin to look for him. And in any case, she couldn't go far with nothing but the few pengős she'd persuaded Zsóka to give her before she left.

She was frightened and forlorn. Out in the streets again, she began to wander in a desultory fashion through the city, trying to work out a plan, trying to think of friends she could turn to. Meanwhile it was getting dark. She was very cold and her feet were growing more and more painful.

Then she recollected an arrangement made between her and her mother, some time before, in the event of their becoming separated from each other. There was a married couple in Pest, trustworthy friends, who had been recommended to Margit by the Mandels. Margit had told Marietta to memorize their name and address, for that would be their meeting point. Marietta wasn't sure of the address anymore, but she thought she still knew the phone number.

She walked on until, at last, she spotted a phone booth on a street corner. She took one of Zsóka's coins from her pocket and dialled the number. A man answered and, hesitantly, she inquired about her mother.

'Is that you, Marietta?' the man asked. 'Thank God! Your mother's been dreadfully worried about you. She's here – you had better talk to her.'

A moment later Margit came on the line. 'Marietta! Where are you?'

'I'm in the inner city, near Váci Street. I've been walking all day, and my feet are bleeding . . .'

'Go to the corner of Váci Street and Régi Pósta Street. We will meet you there in quarter of an hour.'

When Margit left Vali's house that afternoon, a few hours after her daughter, she went straight to this couple's flat in Pest. She was distraught over her daughter's disappearance and had no idea whether the girl remembered the necessary details of their pre-arranged meeting place. She had been waiting and waiting, praying for some sign of Marietta.

They picked her up by car and took her back to the flat. But the two refugees could not stay long with these friends of the Mandels: it wasn't a safe place to hide. So Margit telephoned someone else she knew she could trust: an elderly ex-general, Dezső's former partner in an import-export business. He said they should come at once.

The ex-general and his wife greeted them warmly and welcomed them into a sumptuous apartment, filled with beautiful furniture and antiques. There was obviously plenty of room for an extra couple of people. A lavish supper was served. Their hosts' lives seemed untouched by the horrors and deprivations of the war.

But Margit and Marietta were disappointed when the ex-general said they could stay only one night. The next day they would have to leave. They explained that their servants could not be completely trusted; they would doubtless be suspicious of the new 'guests', and might even denounce them.

So, early the next morning, Margit and her daughter moved on. After a lot of anxious deliberation, Margit finally decided to seek the assistance of their old family lawyer. He was their last hope. And that was when they struck lucky.

The lawyer acted without delay. That same morning he took Marietta to his mother's house on the outskirts of the city, where, in safety and comfort, she was to spend the rest of the war. Then he returned for Margit.

He escorted her to the flat of a friend who was already providing a haven for a large Jewish family. There were sixteen people altogether, living in three rooms on the first floor of an apartment building in Buda. On the third floor of the same building, the Wehrmacht had an office. All day long they heard the stomping of soldiers' boots on the stairs – up and down, up and down. It was a little too close for comfort. But there was

143

also a great advantage in sharing premises with the Wehrmacht: it prevented the Arrow Cross gangs from storming in, as they did elsewhere, in their ceaseless quest for more Jews to murder. The officers of the Wehrmacht provided what little restraining force existed in the capital in those days.

On Christmas Eve the soldiers at the office were informed that Budapest was surrounded by the Red Army. Within minutes they evacuated the building. Margit and the others now sat tight and awaited the inevitable: the ensuing Siege and the defeat of the Occupation forces. Their Christmas present would be a little late, but they had faith that it would come – deliverance.

In February, when it was all over, Margit began her search for Péter. She knew nothing, as yet, about the way in which Dezső had carelessly betrayed his son's whereabouts to the Gestapo. She only knew that the people who had been taking care of him had vanished and her son had vanished with them. Was he still alive?

Crossing into Pest by boat, she inquired at the Red Cross, at hospitals and at the Jewish Rescue Committee. The courtyard of the main synagogue in Dohány Street, in the ghetto, was filled with several hundred corpses of Jewish men, women and children who had either been murdered or had starved to death. They were laid in neat rows so that their families and friends could recognize them. Péter was not among them.

There were thousands more Jewish dead scattered through-out Budapest. It wasn't possible to examine them all. Almost two weeks went by. Her inquiries proved fruitless but she continued the quest for her son, refusing to believe that she would never see him again.

Then she was informed about a Jewish orphanage in the ghetto in which a small boy, who for many weeks had been suffering from a severe case of chicken pox, kept repeating the same singular request: over and over again the child asked to be taken to '106 Andrássy Avenue'. No one paid much attention to this, until a woman working at the orphanage recognized the address as that of the Herzog family and realized that he could be Margit's son.

Péter was in a sorry state when Margit found him. He had survived the appalling conditions of the ghetto (where the police had deposited him after he failed to recognize Vali at the Majestic), but only just. He had not only been starving all that winter but had suffered from frostbite and lost one of his toes.

When Marietta eventually returned from her refuge on the outskirts, she instinctively made her way back to 106 Andrássy Avenue. She stared in disbelief – their old family residence had not outlasted the bombing; it lay in ruins. But she was told by a neighbour that the Herzogs' former caretaker was living at another residence just down the street. Marietta went to see him. Overjoyed to find that she was still alive, he took her in, fed her and gave her shelter. And it was there, soon afterwards, that she and her mother were reunited.

After the war, when Margit's brothers and mother, along with nearly all the other 600,000 Jews deported from the Hungarian countryside during the spring and summer of 1944, failed to come back, she was gradually forced to concede that they were dead. The full story of the extermination camps began to emerge and it was almost impossible to believe.

She learned that the postcard sent by Feri from the innocent-sounding 'Waldsee' was part of the common Nazi procedure of deluding those still at home. Often within minutes of writing them, the deportees were herded into the gas chamber. She found out that Sándor, before being put into the cattle train with the others, was beaten almost to death by gendarmes trying to make him reveal the whereabouts of the family jewellery. He refused. He was gassed on arrival at Auschwitz, along with his mother and brother Gyuri.

Feri, however, managed to stay alive until the Russians reached Auschwitz the following January. He was lying in the camp hospital – the sick inmates there were the only ones not to have been evacuated by the retreating Germans. But he was too ill by then, and he died soon after liberation.

Of the once large and flourishing Herzog family, the only ones left were Imre, who'd been saved by friends in Budapest, and Margit.

With a sorrowful heart, the widow began to build a new life

for herself and her children.

★

When Ilona and the Mandels left Budakeszi Avenue, one by
one, after the raid, they had arranged to meet at Bandi
Schreiber's flat in Madách Square, in Pest. He had helped them
before; now they had no choice but to turn to him again.
Schreiber, a Jew, was still living at home with his Christian
wife, in a yellow star house.

They stayed the night there and the following day Bandi
secured a new refuge for his cousin Jenő and Szerén, in the cellar
of a friend's house. He had a different solution for Ilona. His
contacts in the Jewish underground provided her with a new
identity and forged documents in a matter of hours. She became
Karolin Farkas, a displaced Transylvanian. And on Bandi's
advice, 'Karolin' duly moved into the home of a Christian
woman, a friend who was also well known to the Mandels as a
frequent customer at their shops.

The woman and her two daughters lived in a flat in a heavily
Arrow Cross–inhabited part of Buda. In this building, too, first
the Wehrmacht, then the SS had quarters and an office. Ilona
was young and attractive and appealed to the German occupants. They joked and flirted with her. She spoke perfect
German and when Russian planes dropped propaganda leaflets
urging the people of Budapest to surrender their city and so
avoid its complete destruction, they asked 'Karolin' to translate
the message for them.

During the Siege, they were appalled to find that they were
directly in the front line. They were battered from all sides and
for six weeks Ilona and the others barely left the cellar. The SS
began to panic. Many of them tried to escape from the area
dressed as civilians and they broke into all the flats in the
building to take men's clothing.

Quite suddenly, one morning in mid-February, Ilona and her
friend noticed that the SS had fled. At half-past ten they saw
Russian patrols coming down their street.

Two days later Ilona ventured out to find her parents, who
had been hiding in a flat in another part of Buda. It took her a

146

long time to walk there; after sitting in the cellar for so long, her legs were very weak. She reached the flat only to find it ransacked and empty. Her mother's dressing gown lay on the floor amongst smashed things. Ilona feared the worst.

But a neighbour told her that her parents had departed in a hurry – they'd been evacuated to Csepel, an island on the Danube at the southern end of the city. Ilona made her way to the address she'd been given. Csepel was a long way off. Her legs were now giving way and her feet were sore and blistered. When she reached her destination, her parents were not there. No one could tell her what had happened to them.

She managed to get on to a boat which was taking a few others across to Pest. Exhausted by now, and agonizing over the fate of her parents, she returned to the place where she had been in hiding the previous summer, in case there was a message for her. But there was nothing, So finally, summoning her last drop of strength, she decided to go back to her own home, the flat in Rákóczi Avenue which she had left so long ago in the care of their Christian family housekeeper.

She opened the front door. There in the sitting room, all safe and fit, were her parents, Szerén, Jenő, several other members of the family, and her labour-serviceman husband, who had come back to Budapest on the tide of the Red Army. The flat was in perfect order. The housekeeper had done her job well.

The man who had done so much to help them – Bandi Schreiber, was not so fortunate. After evading capture for so long, he was killed by the rampaging Arrow Cross in the final days before the liberation of Pest.

Forty-five years later, Ilona, a subdued, straight-backed widow, described an incident which took place while she was living as 'Karolin Farkas' in that SS-infested house in Buda.

'I had been doing a few errands and was on my way home. Suddenly I became aware of a man walking some distance behind me. Each street I turned into, he turned into as well. It became apparent that he was following me. I started to panic. What did he want? Was it someone who had recognized me, who knew that I was not a Christian from Transylvania, but a Jew?

147

'We got closer and closer to the house. He had now been walking behind me for half an hour. I was almost paralysed with fear, convinced that the man would follow me straight to my door and denounce me then and there as a Jew, and the Germans at the house would drag me away, shoot me, deport me, God only knew what.

'I reached the house, hurried through the entrance and fled into our flat. I locked the door behind me and then, trembling with my back against the wall, I waited for the inevitable, too frightened to speak. My friend stared at me, shocked and bewildered. Then we heard the knock on the door.

'She opened the door and it was him, the man who'd just been following me. "Excuse me," he said, "I don't wish to disturb you. But I'm responsible for water distribution in this building, and I want to know whether you have enough for now or would like me to bring you another bucketful."

'And he was speaking the truth. He lived right there, in one of the flats downstairs. The man hadn't been following me at all, but simply taking the same route home.

'That episode has stayed with me all these years. I still have nightmares about being followed by some strange, sinister person, someone who is about to betray me. And even when I don't have nightmares, I never sleep very well. I haven't had one unbroken night's sleep from that day to this.'

*

Eventually, too, Vali found someone who could tell her a little about the fate of Paul Engel, the Jewish landowner with whom she'd had her first serious love affair when she finished her studies. They had lost contact with each other three years earlier. When Vali last met him, he was still dividing his time between his baroque castle in Dormánd and his hilltop flat overlooking Budapest, still driving his sports car and surrounding himself with pretty women.

In 1942, like so many thousands of other Jewish men, Engel was called into the labour service. Many of these forced labour servicemen were dispatched to the Eastern Front, together with the Second Hungarian Army, and the majority perished in the winter of 1942–3, when the Red Army broke through the Axis lines at the River Don.

Perhaps Engel was killed then. Or perhaps he survived the Front, and was among those labour servicemen later sent to the notorious Bor copper mines in Serbia, where most succumbed to the inhuman treatment and conditions. Finally, at the end of 1944 and the beginning of 1945, those who were still alive after these years of torment were made to march endless miles to Mauthausen or Dachau, where only a handful survived. A lover of literature, Engel might have spent some time together with the poet Miklós Radnóti, who survived the atrocities of the Bor mines only to be shot when he finally collapsed on the road to Mauthausen. He was buried in a mass grave, but soon after the war his corpse was dug up again, and there, decaying in the pocket of his uniform, was the notebook into which he had written his last poems. They were published in a slim volume under the title *Bor Notebook*.

But Engel might also have been killed by one of the many sadistic Hungarian military guards put in charge of labour service battalions; they had been advised by their superiors to 'bring back as few Jews as possible'. (Vilmos Nagybaczoni-Nagy, Defence Minister in the Kállay government, was appalled when he visited the Front and saw how harshly they were treated. He and Kállay tried to foster a more humane attitude towards the Jewish labour servicemen. Those servicemen who had remained on Hungarian soil fared much better. But anti-Semitism of the most vicious kind was too in-built in the Hungarian military structure at that time, and the influence of the SS was too great. The Kállay government was unable to stop the brutality.)

Vali never found out how or where Paul Engel died. He never came back from the labour service – that was all anyone knew. The refined landowner who, a decade earlier, had swept her away to Monte Carlo and the French Riviera, who had revealed to her the delights of the poet Villon and given her her first taste of romance, was last seen marching away with his labour battalion, wearing ragged trousers and a pair of battered wooden clogs.

*

The war had created a tragic void around Vali. So many of the people who had been close and important to her had died: her constant champion Barabás, Engel, Sándor Herzog, Bandi Schreiber – her old employer from the Transylvanian summers – and her trusted *couturier* Sándor Gergely, who had committed suicide. Many other Jewish friends and associates – composers and musicians, writers, film and theatre people – had perished. There was an eerie silence in Vali's life.

She could feel that something irreversible had taken place. The foundations on which she had built her life and career had disappeared beneath her. A whole era had been swept away by history – the era which had seen her rise to fame and embodied her glorious heyday. Nothing would ever be the same, she could never be that kind of star again. Symbolically, her unique and beloved Hangli, where for six years she had reigned as undisputed queen, lay in the dust.

She felt very alone, for the first time in her life. And she, too, was changed. Something vital had left her. She was spiritually, emotionally and physically impoverished.

Paul Barabás

Margit Herzog with
Marietta and Péter in 1942

Dezső Keleti on his return from
labour service – the torment shows in his eyes

Jenő and Szerén Mandel

Vera Somló in 1944

Admiral Nicholas Horthy
[photo: MTI, Budapest]

Szálasi, in foreground, takes over in October 1944.
Defence Minister Beregfy is second from the left [photo: MTI, Budapest]

The Siege rages on the streets of Budapest — the winter of 1944/5
[photo: MTI, Budapest]

Péter Hain, in handcuffs, being led away by Gábor Péter, on his
return to Hungary to stand trial as a war criminal, 1945

Sasha (with bandaged head) and Lajos Esküdt
outside Vali's house, March 1945

Péter Halász in 1946

Married life

The family at home in pre-Revolution days — the author is
sitting on her mother's lap; brother Valér is standing

The headmaster's house in Gölle, as it is today

The Majestic as it is today — a dilapidated apartment building

Péter Halász in the 1980s

Vali Rácz makes her comeback: in a Budapest radio station, 1988

Thirteen

When Baroness Kóhner's apartment in Pest had been repaired and redecorated, she and her family left 47d Budakeszi Avenue. By now they had been there for four months and Vali was unashamedly relieved to see them go. All at once there was an unaccustomed tranquillity in the house. For the past year it had been filled to bursting point – with Jews, Russians, displaced aristocrats and others in need of asylum. Now there was only Vali, Aunt Karolin and her husband Lajos.

It was into this strange new calm that one night, out of nowhere, Sasha appeared. Vali arrived home from the Café de la Paix to find his jeep outside the house and Sasha waiting for her by the baby grand in the sitting room.

'I told you I would come back one more time, to say goodbye.'

After mopping up in Germany, he and his men were passing through Hungary on their way home. They had won the war, the great and victorious Red Army, and they were returning to the Soviet Union as heroes. But Sasha's face looked worn and tired, not victorious. He too, like Vali, had been drained by the war.

He told her he was billeted for the night in a small village outside Budapest and asked whether she would spend the night with him there. She tossed a nightgown and a few other things into a bag and they drove off in his jeep.

He had a room in a peasant house. It was large and comfortable, furnished in typical Magyar folk style. There they spent their last hours of passion.

Afterwards, Sasha sat beside her as she lay on the bed. For a long time he studied her in silence. His eyes were sorrowful and pensive.

'Tell me,' Vali asked, 'what does your Stalin look like? I've never seen a picture of him.'

There was a Russian newspaper on the table. Sasha picked it up and found the obligatory photograph of the dictator on one of its pages. He showed it to her.

'He doesn't seem so bad,' she observed. 'He looks rather like a smiling grandpa.'

Sasha made no comment. He folded the paper and put it away.

He didn't feel like talking that night. He held her hand, stroked her hair, and looked at her, endlessly, as though he were filling himself with the sight of her, because after that night, he knew he could never see her again.

The next morning he drove her back home. He went into the house briefly, to bid farewell to the Esküdts. Then Vali walked with him to the front gate. The parting was painful for her, because she had genuine deep feelings for the man who had not only helped her through a desperate time but had saved her life. And it was even more painful for Sasha. For Vali was so clearly the love of his life.

He clasped her hands tightly, and kissed them. Then he got into the jeep, next to his old driver. As it left the kerb, he waved and gave her a last smile. It was the smile of a man filled with an infinite sadness. Vali watched from the gate until the jeep drove out of view.

She never knew what became of him, once he had been swallowed up again by his vast and impenetrable country. But it might please him to know, if he is still alive, that the image of his departure – the look in his eyes, the smile and that wave – had engraved itself so firmly in her mind, that four and a half decades have done nothing to obscure it.

★

The engagement at the Café de la Paix finished in August, and afterwards Vali was invited to appear at many of the other cafés, restaurants and nightclubs re-opening during that summer and autumn. They had French names – the Moulin Rouge, the Café de Paris, the Parisette.

Her show at the Parisette, in Vörösmarty Square, a stone's throw from the Vigadó concert hall and the site of the Hangli, was titled *New Songs for New Times*.

New times indeed. Everything had been turned on its head. Those who'd once had Vali at their mercy, now appealed to her for help.

A plaintive-sounding woman rang one day, whose voice was vaguely familiar. She explained that her fiancé was in trouble and that only Vali could get him out of it.

'Who is your fiancé?'

'I'm sure you will remember him, *művésznő*, he was one of the detectives at the Majestic. You were often called in to see him. He was kind to you – gave you coffee, and cake. A well-mannered young man, not really like a detective at all. His real passion is for singing. The two of you had many talks about classical music.'

Vali recalled the 'tenor-interrogator' who had seemed so uninterested in whether or not she'd been hiding Jews. 'Well, what can I do?'

'He's been arrested. Of course, it's true that he worked for the Arrow Cross. But he was not a cruel man. He never tortured anyone. Please put in a good word for him.'

Vali promised to do what she could. 'And who are you? Do we know each other?'

There was a slight pause on the line. 'Yes, you know me. I was at the Majestic, too. I'm the woman who used to sit beside you on the bench. We chatted sometimes.'

The young blonde who had befriended her and tried to win her confidence. 'We're both Christian,' she had said, 'we should stick together.' Vali had assumed correctly that she was an informer. She had tried to do her boyfriend's job for him.

Some time later there was another phone call, from the guard at the Majestic who had, on her first night there, given her his fur-lined leather gloves to use as a pillow. It had been a rare act of kindness. Now he, too, was in trouble. To have been a

153

low-ranking employee of the Gestapo was not a good character reference in the eyes of the post-war Communist-led regime. (Although, with typical Stalinist irony, other, more overt Fascists were often considered perfect cadre-material.) Vali agreed to speak in the former guard's defence. In due course she was summoned by the authorities and her testimony helped to mitigate his sentence.

Vali received yet another call (perhaps the most surprising one) from Marika. The gold-toothed bombshell, who'd had such a good time with the 'Ivans' in Vali's basement, spoke in a new, strident tone. The niece of the former Arrow Cross bigwig informed Vali that she had recently joined the Communist Party. She had plans and ambitions.

'And you had better not hinder me,' she threatened. 'I would advise you to tell no one about my uncle, or that my family had any connections whatsoever with the Szálasi government. I could make things very unpleasant for you. Have I made myself clear?'

They were new times, all right.

Fourteen

Despite the subversive activities and the camouflaged power-wielding of the Communists, the municipal elections held in Budapest on 7 October 1945 were won with an absolute majority by the Smallholders' Party. It was a remarkable demonstration of the Magyar people's deep-seated desire for democracy. The Communists, who had expected to be swept into power through the support of the working-class districts of the capital, were flabbergasted. They redoubled their efforts to secure victory in the November general election. Their many advantages made them supremely confident. Not only were they backed by the omnipotent occupation forces, and able to organize instant 'mass demonstrations', but, in contrast to the non-Communist parties, they had transportation facilities and the media at their disposal.

The Russians allocated all newsprint, and the publication of newspapers was authorized by a licensing system. Very few political groups, besides the Communist and Socialist parties, were permitted to publish newspapers. And the printers, whose trade union was one of the first to be penetrated by the Communists, refused to publish articles which the Communist Party objected to.

But despite all this, they again failed dismally in the general election on 4 November, polling a mere seventeen per cent of the votes. The Smallholders won nearly sixty per cent of the seats in Parliament. It was clear proof that the Communists had been unable to attract the confidence and the support of the one

155

class that had been their greatest hope: the agrarian proletariat. Now they were really galled. The Party's General Secretary, Rákosi, was compelled to go to Moscow to make excuses.

The new Government was led by Zoltán Tildy, a Smallholder and Calvinist pastor. And it was at first agreed that the crucial Interior Ministry should be held by a member of the victorious Smallholders. But a few days later ACC Chairman Marshal Voroshilov vetoed this decision. And Rákosi, who was to become a vice-premier in the new government, told the baffled Smallholders: 'You don't seem to understand the situation. Look around you in Eastern Europe. Do you see a single country in which the Interior Ministry is not in the hands of the Communist Party?' The Smallholders gave in. They held an impressive number of cabinet seats, but not the positions of real power.

The Communists were now ready for the next step – to isolate the Smallholders' Party. Together with the Socialists, the 'fellow traveller' Peasant Party and the Trade Union Council, they formed a leftist bloc within the government, and proceeded to propel the entire machinery leftwards. The bloc, claiming to speak 'in the name of the Hungarian people', threatened and coerced the Smallholders. Politicians opposing the demands of the bloc were branded as 'fascists' and 'enemies of the people'. Parliament was thus unable to exercise its normal democratic functions.

It was the beginning of the irreversible process by which the Communists would soon liquidate all opposition. Hungary's infant democracy was being strangled at birth.

★

Side by side with the unfolding political plot was the drama of the return of Hungary's war criminals. On a chilly, drizzly morning at the beginning of October, a group of them were flown to Mátyásföld Airport on the outskirts of Budapest by the US Army, from the military camp in Austria where they had been held since the end of the war. As they got off the plane, the returning criminals were met by Gábor Péter, chief of the political police, and handcuffs.

156

Among the eleven prisoners were two of the country's former prime ministers, Béla Imrédy and László Bárdossy, and the self-styled 'Leader of the Nation', Ferenc Szálasi. The group also included László Endre, who (together with László Baky) was one of the two state secretaries in Sztójay's quisling government who had helped Eichmann implement his deportation programme, and Andor Jaross and Lajos Reményi-Schneller, Sztójay's Interior Minister and Finance Minister, respectively. All were loaded into a police van and driven to ÁVO headquarters at 60 Andrássy Avenue, where they were locked in the same subterranean cells formerly used by the Arrow Cross to hold *their* political prisoners.

Each new prisoner was taken for initial questioning to the office occupied by Gábor Péter. Hanging on the wall behind Péter's desk was a huge photograph of the ruins of Budapest's famous Chain Bridge, blown up by the Nazis during the Siege. It was, unavoidably, the first thing anyone saw on entering the room. And Péter's opening query to each prisoner was, 'What do you say to this picture? How do you feel about the destruction of Budapest?'

Péter, a former tailor's assistant who had emigrated years earlier to the Soviet Union, belonged to the inner circle of Muscovites who had come back to Hungary with the Red Army, in which he held the rank of colonel. He was the central figure in the prosecution of the war criminals and claimed to have 'the interests of the young Hungarian democracy' at heart.

Nearly 59,000 people were to stand trial for war crimes in the years following the Second World War. Of these, 26,286 were found guilty. The majority were small fry, and were sentenced to varying terms of imprisonment or confiscation of property. Others were sentenced to life imprisonment or hard labour, or both. But in that harsh winter of 1945–6, when the major criminals were tried by the new Hungarian People's Court in the auditorium of the Music Academy, the death sentence was passed in 189 cases, and carried out either by firing squad or hanging.

The two Lászlós, Baky and Endre, took their last walk to the gallows within minutes of each other, cronies to the end. Péter

Hain, Eichmann's side-kick at the Hotel Majestic, was also returned to Hungary and sentenced to death, but before the sentence could be carried out he killed himself by jumping from a third floor window of 60 Andrássy Avenue. Arrow Cross Interior Minister Gábor Vajna, who had herded the Jews into the ghetto, was hanged. The three ex-prime ministers – Bárdossy, Imrédy and Sztójay – were given the privilege of death by firing squad.

The quisling, Sztójay (who'd once remarked that he had more faith in German victory than even Hitler), was condemned for obvious reasons, although during his term in office the real power had lain more in the hands of Edmund Veesenmayer, Reich Plenipotentiary in Hungary. Veesenmayer was sentenced to twenty years in prison by the International War Crimes Tribunal at Nüremberg, but he served a mere three years of his sentence before being set free.

Bárdossy was condemned for committing the major blunder of declaring war first on the Soviet Union, and then on the United States, thereby ensuring the downfall and decimation of his country. Imrédy's crime had been to set Hungary on the road to catastrophe in the first place by passing anti-Jewish legislation and bringing the country deeper into the Nazi orbit. He had also been a keen supporter of the Sztójay government, putting at its disposal his undisputed intellectual prowess.

Neither Bárdossy nor Imrédy were prepared to admit to any guilt on their part. Imrédy spoke eloquently in his own defence. Asked how he could have been so confident of his actions *vis-à-vis* the Nazis, he replied, 'Anyone who, tumbling down the Niagara Falls of history, or caught in an earthquake's catharsis, does not believe that he is right, will go under.' His final, sardonic statement to the court was, 'Personally, I wouldn't have condemned myself to death.' They faced the firing squad (Imrédy with a handkerchief over his eyes, Bárdossy with eyes open) convinced of their innocence. Sztójay, though, was full of remorse, and said that with hindsight he would have acted differently.

Father Kun made a meticulous list of all his bloodthirsty deeds in a lengthy document written in prison. He was calmly repentant, explaining how his atrocities began in early December, when the Arrow Cross civil and military leadership fled the city before the advancing Russians. With no one to restrain them, and inspired by the outpouring of Nazi propaganda in the press and on the radio, they became drunk with their own power. He ended with the words: '. . . with broken heart and soul, I confess before God and Man, and beg everyone's forgiveness.'

Several high-ranking army officers were sentenced to death. Ferenc Feketehalmy-Czeydner, Márton Zöldy and József Grassy were found guilty of inciting the mass murder in January 1942 of 2,000 Serbians and 1,000 Jewish men, women and children in Ujvidék (Novi Sad), in the Serbian region awarded to Hungary for its part in the 1941 invasion of Yugoslavia. They justified the massacre by claiming to have put down a 'partisan revolt'. The three officers were tried in Hungary, then handed over to the Yugoslavs, who hanged them.

Ferenc Szombathelyi and Gusztáv Jány were among those held responsible for the tremendous losses of the Second Hungarian Army on the Eastern Front in 1942–3. At the end of each war-crimes trial, after judgement was passed, those sentenced to death were asked whether they wished to put in a plea for mercy. Jány was the only one to decline. 'I do not ask for mercy, because by doing so I would be admitting guilt.'

By contrast, the former Arrow Cross Defence Minister, Károly Beregfy, displayed a cowardly streak in his final hours. This strong-arm man had previously ordered all army deserters, traitors and political opponents to be instantly and brutally put to death – drawn and quartered by the sword or else hanged. On the night before his execution he said he had a last request and asked for the executioner to come to his cell. After a few minutes the executioner came out laughing. When he was asked what had taken place, he replied that Beregfy had wanted him to ensure that his death would be painless. He was prepared to give him anything in return. 'What have you got left to give me?' the executioner asked with wry humour. Beregfy pointed to his lace-up army boots, still in good condition. 'You can take these, if you promise I will die without pain.'

159

But the most pathetic case was that of Szálasi. He was unrepentant to the end, considering himself a blameless patriot. Even after he had been sentenced to death by hanging, he was convinced that he was so well-loved by 'the people', that they would not allow him to die. He was sure that at the last moment his loyal supporters would rush up to him and set him free.

When Szálasi stepped out through the prison door into the courtyard containing the gallows, flanked by two guards, he seemed proud and confident, his head held high. But as soon as the crowd saw him, they began to scream at him in a frenzy of bitterness and hatred. 'Murderer! Scoundrel! Bloodthirsty criminal!' He took two steps forward, then he seemed to collapse. The guards on either side of him had to prop him up and so lead him to the gallows. As they placed the rope around his neck, his expression revealed that at long last, in the final moment of his life, he abandoned his delusions.

Admiral Nicholas Horthy, who for twenty-five years had led his nation through times of both hope and despair, never stood trial in Hungary. The Hungarian authorities tried, but failed to persuade the Americans to extradite him after the war. The Americans undoubtedly saved his life by this action, for the People's Court would have shown little mercy towards the 'feudal lord' who had been the scourge of the Communists and had kowtowed to Hitler.

To the Americans, though, he was the elder statesman who had repeatedly attempted to disentangle his hapless nation from the Axis cords which bound it. His sin was that he simply wasn't up to the task.

*

Budapest's reconstruction after the war would take decades. Once-beautiful vistas were replaced by views of rubble-strewn bomb sites. Buildings stood gutted and abandoned. Houses everywhere were disfigured by artillery shells and machine-gun fire. The last of the bridges to be rebuilt was finished in 1963, and the restoration of the Castle was completed only in the early 1980s.

A few short years after the war, Berlin – the capital of Nazism, seat of the 'thousand-year Reich', home to millions of Hitler's adoring fans – stood anew. West Berlin rose from the dust in all its glorious prosperity. But Budapest, the sacrifice to Hitler's demented dreams, would never recover completely.

Some months after the war, though, an extraordinary event took place. As the city's only bridge across the Danube was the Russian pontoon bridge, it was decided that a second, permanent bridge would have to be built immediately in order to facilitate essential communication between Buda and Pest. It would have to be completed before winter set in and the river froze over, making construction impossible.

An army of workmen was culled from the population of the capital. They had a very difficult job, because few of the necessary tools were available. And as there was a severe food shortage at the time, the workers were ill-fed. Their sustenance came mainly from the assortment of food parcels donated by the people of Budapest. Dressed in rags and weary from overwork, the men nevertheless managed to complete the Kossuth Bridge opposite Parliament in a temperature of ten degrees below zero, on the very day that ice began to form on the river.

A famous play by the then-Communist writer, Gyula Háy, was written about this admirable feat and put on at Budapest's National Theatre. *The Bridge of Life* was full of symbolism about the hopeful future made possible by courtesy of Mr Stalin, and the deeply humane and heroic acts which were inspired by Communist guidance.

The city's shopkeepers and businessmen had been encouraged by the government to put their savings into the construction of the bridge. Many of them did. After the Communist take-over in 1948, these same people had their businesses expropriated without compensation.

★

In January 1946, Vali Rácz went to the Japán Coffee House on Andrássy Avenue, where she had an appointment with the theatre director Gábor Békefy. They were to discuss the new

161

variety show he was staging, in which Békefy wanted her to sing. The Japán was an elegant nineteenth-century establishment, famous for its artistic and literary clientele.

Vali was not at her most seductive. She had just returned from a visit to Gölle. The annual pig-slaughter had just taken place and, through a friend in the military, she had been given special authority to bring two whole pigs' carcasses back to Budapest, as well as a lot of other provisions. Two soldiers had driven her down to Gölle and back in an army lorry. She was wearing a long sheepskin coat and lace-up boots, had a scarf around her head, and was weary from the long drive.

She spotted Gábor sitting with an unfamiliar young man at one of the marble-topped tables, waved and made her way towards them.

'My dear Vali,' Gábor began, 'let me introduce you to a friend of mine – the writer, Péter Halász.'

They shook hands. Vali was instantly attracted to the handsome writer with the dark eyes and hair. And he was thrilled to make her acquaintance. Several years her junior, he'd known her only as an inaccessible star of the Hungarian cinema and popular music scene.

Péter Halász had made his name with his first novel, published in 1941, when he was only nineteen. His national reputation was further established with his second book, the following year. Then the war intervened. In 1943 he was sent to the Front in Eastern Hungary. He escaped from his battalion only to fall into Russian hands and end up in a Soviet POW camp in the Ukraine. He then joined a unit of volunteers to fight the Germans in Berlin, but fell critically ill with jaundice, spent a month in hospital and, by a stroke of luck, returned to his native Budapest on the same day that the war was over in Hungary – 4 April 1945.

Now he was enthusiastically resuming the career which had been so abruptly cut off, and writing his first three-act stage play.

Six months later he and Vali were married: Gábor Békefy was one of the witnesses at the ceremony.

Fifteen

Hungary was proclaimed a republic on 1 February 1946. Almost immediately the Communists claimed to have unearthed a large-scale 'conspiracy' against the fledgling republic. According to Communist newspapers, the Smallholders' Party was behind this conspiracy. One of the Smallholders' cabinet ministers and several other members of the Party were arrested and 'confessions' extracted from them.

The confessions implicated Béla Kovács, General Secretary of the Smallholders, who then testified before the political police. He was arrested by Soviet authorities on 25 February and charged with espionage against the Soviet Army.

In April the People's Court sentenced three of the alleged conspirators to death, the others to long prison terms. In the middle of May, Prime Minister Ferenc Nagy, worn out by the crisis, left for a holiday in Switzerland. While he was away, more of the leading Smallholders, including the Prime Minister himself, were implicated in the conspiracy.

When Nagy was informed of this, he planned to return at once to defend himself. But friends in Budapest advised him against it; his life would be in danger. Bitterly disappointed, he resigned at the end of May and remained in exile. Another Smallholder leader, President of Parliament Monseigneur Béla Varga, was forced to flee Hungary a few days later in order to avoid arrest.

The Smallholder leadership had been effectively liquidated. The Party's remaining members in Parliament had no genuine

163

voice of opposition; they were compelled to submit totally to the Communist will. And the appointment of the new Prime Minister, Lajos Dinnyés, was engineered by Marshal Voroshilov's deputy. So the Smallholders had in essence been absorbed into the powerful leftist bloc.

The stage was set for the next act: the general election of August 1947. Six opposition parties had been authorized by the Allied Control Commission, who wanted to give the whole affair the semblance of genuine parliamentary democracy. But the Communists felt sure they would wipe the floor with this weak and hastily-established opposition.

Zoltán Pfeiffer, expelled from the Smallholders, had recently founded the Independence Party. He was seen as a potentially effective adversary, and so the Communists concentrated their campaign of terror and vilification against him and his new party. They dismissed the five other opposition parties, considering them too disorganized, lacking in effective leadership and funds, and too intimidated to pose a threat.

Once again, they were wrong. Despite the widespread electoral frauds organized by László Rajk, the Communist Interior Minister, whereby Communists were secretly able to vote ten to twenty times, and many non-Communists were illegally barred from voting altogether, they did poorly in the election. The four parties of the leftist coalition barely obtained a majority. The Communists won only twenty-two per cent of the votes.

Two of the opposition parties, the Democratic People's Party (a Catholic organization) and Pfeiffer's Independence Party, did amazingly well. They ended up with sixty and forty-nine seats in Parliament respectively.

Giorgi Pushkin, Russian Minister in Hungary, observed acidly that the Hungarian people did not seem to appreciate the many generous gestures made by the Soviet Union.

The Communists had had enough. They now determined to destroy even the appearance of parliamentarianism.

The forty-nine members of the Independence Party were labelled 'fascists' and deprived of their seats in the National Assembly. Its leader, Pfeiffer, like others before him, was forced to flee the country. Within a year the other major opposition party, the Democratic People's, had been dissolved, and its leader, István Barankovics, also escaped to the West.

On 30 July 1948, the President of the Republic, Zoltán Tildy, was forced to resign. He was succeeded by Socialist Árpád Szakasits, who was mainly a spokesman for Mátyás Rákosi. Whenever he did oppose the Communists, under pressure from independent-minded Socialists, he was branded a 'rightist deviationist' by the Communist press.

One purge followed another, until only Communist stooges and fellow travellers were left. Then the Socialists and Communists merged into the new Hungarian Workers' Party. All independent parties ceased to exist. Hungary became a People's Republic.

Attacks against the Catholic Church and Cardinal Mindszenty were intensified, on the grounds that the Church was protecting reactionaries. The Cardinal was arrested in December and sentenced to life imprisonment.

The Communist newspaper *Szabad Nép* (Free People) described 1948 as 'the year of victories'.

Everything was now ready for the grand finale: the Stalinist show trials of 1949, when the Communist Party itself would be purged in order to demonstrate, once and for all, to anyone who still entertained doubts, that not the slightest breach of discipline would be tolerated by the real master of Hungary: Joseph Stalin.

Rákosi claimed to have discovered yet another 'conspiracy'. Marshal Tito of Yugoslavia had earlier rebelled and broken away from the Soviet orbit, and to be accused of 'Titoism' had become the most heinous crime in the Muscovite vocabulary. Now Rákosi claimed that there was a Titoist conspiracy brewing at the heart of the government of the Hungarian People's Democracy.

Stalin was eager to strengthen his control over his newly acquired satellite states, to cement his empire together. The show trials were the most effective way to deter any of these states from following the Yugoslav example and producing their own home-grown, independent brand of Communism.

There would have to be a single, direct chain of command from Moscow to Budapest – from Stalin to Rákosi – and no one must be allowed to interfere with it. So the sacrificial lambs would clearly have to be those Hungarian Communists who had not been trained in Moscow, the 'outsiders', for no matter how loyal they were to Stalin now, one day their nationalism might get the better of them and they might resist the direct chain of command.

László Rajk, the ruthless Interior Minister (and later Foreign Minister) who had tried to rig the 1947 election, could hardly be called a 'lamb'. But he was the premier sacrifice, the star of the show trials, because he was the most influential person in the government who was not 'one of them'. Rajk, a veteran of the Spanish Civil War's International Brigade, had not been in Russia during the Second World War, but in Hungary, where he'd been one of the leaders of the Communist underground. He was first imprisoned and then deported to a German concentration camp. He returned to Budapest after the war.

Rajk and many other members of the government were arrested by the ÁVO (by now transformed into the bigger and even more powerful ÁVH) and imprisoned at its headquarters at 60 Andrássy Avenue. And this was when the special talents of secret police chief Gábor Péter really came to the fore. Through the most extraordinarily refined and complex system of torture, coupled with an elaborate web of lies, he was able to force virtually all of these men to confess to being 'Titoist conspirators' – i.e. traitors and spies in the pay of Yugoslavia and various Western countries.

Of course, Péter's domain in Andrássy Avenue had been vastly upgraded since the old 'House of Loyalty' days when it was the Arrow Cross headquarters. It had been expanded from merely one building to an entire block and underneath it all was a vast labyrinthine network of cells and torture rooms. The avenue itself had been renamed People's Republic Avenue.

Under Rákosi's instructions, Interior Minister János Kádár assured Rajk that he was acting in the best interests of the Party by confessing to the charges, and that the sacrifice he was making would be admired by all of his comrades. And Kádár

166

promised that, should he receive the death sentence, it would not be carried out. Rather, he would be spirited away to Russia with his family, where he would be given an important position worthy of his abilities. To Rajk, loyalty to the Party was everything. No sacrifice was too great. So he played their game, putting his faith in Kádár and Rákosi and the men of Moscow.

He was hanged on 15 October 1949.

Several others were hanged with him. And hundreds more were thrown into prison, where they were to rot for years . . . until the death of Stalin.

★

It was in the summer of 1946, with the Communists still mid-stream in their process of hijacking the Hungarian nation and its destiny, that Vali had a surprising encounter one day in downtown Pest.

She had stopped in at the Mandels' store in Váci Street, which had been recently reopened, and was chatting to Szerén, when a woman in her early sixties came in. She was clearly a friend of Szerén's; they greeted each other by first names.

When the woman saw Vali she started, then smiled in recognition. Vali smiled back, thinking that she was merely an admiring member of the public.

'Don't you remember me, *művésznő*?'

Vali stepped a little closer to the woman. 'No,' she apologized. 'Have we met?'

'Yes. We were imprisoned together at the Majestic. I was there with my family – my husband, daughter, son-in-law and small grandchild. You might recall the little boy . . .'

Vali had started a new life since the end of the war. She had married and was looking to the future. Those horrific times from the winter of 1944–5 had to be left behind. She had to try to forget. But now she began to recall the tragic family at the Majestic.

She had seen a young woman, on that first night of her incarceration, dragged into the room by her hair and tossed on to the floor, where she lay, unconscious, beaten almost to

167

death. And the next day she had befriended the parents and the husband of this young woman, whose five-year-old son was there, too – a quiet, frightened, withdrawn child.

The woman at the Mandels' store, the child's grandmother, was the only member of the family still alive. She now told Vali what had happened to them.

In the same group as Vera Somló, they'd been taken away by Kun's men and herded along the Danube embankment. But unlike Vera, who was grudgingly spared just as she was about to be killed, this family was taken one by one (the child, too), and shot into the water. They had all died instantly, except for the grandmother.

Gravely wounded, she was carried downstream for about a kilometre, where she was discovered by some people walking near the river's edge. The sight of bodies being washed downstream was common in those days, but she was still conscious and obviously alive. She was rescued and taken to a doctor.

Her face was etched with terrible pain and suffering, but Vali could see something else there, too. There was a hard, implac-able quality in her eyes which had not been there at the Majestic. She still grieved, but no longer from a position of weakness. She told Vali that, right after the Liberation, she had joined the Communist Party. In less than a year and a half, she had acquired considerable influence and power, having risen to the rank of senior official in the new administration.

Vali understood the woman and why she had been drawn to the Communists; she understood the need for revenge. The Party, the Muscovites, and ultimately, Stalin, gave the grand-mother who had seen her whole family murdered the *raison d'être* without which she could not have carried on. She forged within herself the new ruthlessness demanded.

She had already learned from the Mandels how Vali had helped them survive the Occupation. (For obvious reasons, the subject had never been mentioned at the Majestic.) And she remembered the comfort and support Vali had given her fellow-prisoners, including her own family. Now she wished to return the kindness.

She wrote her telephone number down on a piece of paper and handed it to Vali. 'Who knows, one day you might need my help. Feel free to call me.'

Vali expressed her gratitude, but didn't seriously think she would ever require the woman's help.

Vali eventually forgot her name, and the piece of paper was lost.

Years later, in the blackest days of the Rákosi dictatorship, there were occasions when she wished she'd held on to it, when to have had at least one ally in the Communist power structure would have been helpful indeed. But it was too late by then. Their mutual friends, the Mandels, having had their business nationalized, had already emigrated to Israel. Vali was cut off from them. And they must have been a source of discomfort to the grandmother from the Majestic, because anyone with the slightest foreign connection was regarded as a potential 'imperialist agent'.

★

Stalin died in 1953 and was succeeded six months later by Nikita Khrushchev, who at once ushered in limited political reforms. Deeply critical of the 'cult of personality' practised by his old mentor, Stalin, one of the first things he resolved to do was to dilute authority at the top. Control of the party apparatus was to be separated from leadership in the administration.

His satellites, naturally, were compelled to do likewise. So Rákosi, who was undisputed boss of Hungary, was ordered to delegate authority forthwith. Khrushchev realized that, if left to his own devices, Rákosi would merely divest himself of some of his many offices and hand them over to his puppets. So he was summoned to Moscow and told to bring along two of the Party's mavericks – István Dobi (a former Smallholder turned Communist) and Imre Nagy, only recently reinstated after being condemned for Titoist deviations. Khrushchev's insistence on giving power to these outsiders was a clear indication that changes were to be more than merely cosmetic.

In Moscow, Rákosi's leadership was denounced in no

169

uncertain terms. His agricultural policies had been disastrous. The forced collectivization had caused hundreds of thousands of peasants to abandon the land. And his overweening ambition to build up a great industrial economy under his Five Year Plan of 1950 had failed dismally. The vastly over-manned industries were running at a loss, and the land was without sufficient people to work it. The country lacked food. The Hungarian people were in resentful mood. If things didn't change, warned Khrushchev, his government would be kicked out.

Back in Budapest, Rákosi reluctantly relinquished his premiership to Imre Nagy. They became bitter enemies. Rákosi did everything he could to discredit Nagy and the package of reforms immediately announced by the new Premier: forced collectivization was to be stopped; the peasants would be free to leave the *kolkhozes*, the collective farms, if they wanted; the mistakes of over-industrialization would be corrected and emphasis would be put on the production of more consumer goods.

But most significantly, Nagy promised to abolish police terror and the institutionalized system of arbitrary arrests by which thousands of innocent people had been gaoled on political charges during Rákosi's years in power. He wanted to review the cases of all political prisoners, and release as many as possible. He knew that Khrushchev, who had already brought in a sweeping political amnesty in Russia, would support him in this.

Rákosi fought the policy tooth and nail. He didn't object to the release of the thousands of obscure and harmless political prisoners who'd been languishing in internment camps and gaols throughout the country. But he vehemently resisted the release of those hundreds of people, mainly Communists and social democrats, who had been arrested, tortured and made to sign false confessions during his purges from 1949 to 1952.

Rákosi's interference incensed Khrushchev, who ordered the immediate release and rehabilitation of the victims of the purges. He didn't foresee the enormous (and for him, undesirable) consequences of this action.

Many of those arrested in the purges had been left-wing

intellectuals, writers and journalists. When they were freed, they made every detail of their horrendous tortures and extracted confessions known to their colleagues, those who had been duped into believing that the prisoners had indeed been guilty of crimes against the State. The Communist intellectuals who had remained loyal to Rákosi and the other Muscovites, whose writings had supported the purges and vilified the 'Titoist conspirators', now saw how blind they had been. They felt betrayed and morally degraded. And they were extremely angry.

The rehabilitations were completed by the autumn of 1954, and Nagy's position seemed unassailable. But early the following year a change in the Moscow Politburo resulted in Nagy's sudden fall from favour and his condemnation as a 'rightist deviationist'. He was ousted and expelled from the Party. Rákosi, gloating over his fall, now made a come-back in the eyes of Moscow. But in Hungary he was surrounded by people who hungered for revenge against the tyrant who had persecuted them, who had lied for years, who had brought the country to near-ruin.

Late in 1955 articles criticizing Rákosi began to appear in the *Irodalmi Újság* (Literary Gazette), the official organ of the Writers' Association. It was the beginning of a press campaign against him and his regime, which was to gain impetus over the coming months. It was accompanied by a series of fiery meetings of the Petőfi Circle, a discussion group organized by the Communist Youth League. Imre Nagy, who had tried to humanize the system, became the hero-figure of the country's disillusioned Communists.

In March 1956, Rákosi was forced to concede publicly that Rajk and the others executed with him had been innocent. This lost him his remaining support and authority in both the Party and the country. Moscow, seeing that it would be impossible to try to keep their man in power, decided to let him go. They replaced him with one of his chief associates, Ernő Gerő.

But this was unacceptable to the vast army of opponents of the regime, who were growing more and more outspoken with every day. The rage and rebellion which had begun with the

171

intellectuals was spreading like wildfire throughout society. Factory workers were holding meetings of their own. University students and even schoolchildren were voicing their intense opposition.

The government bureaucracy included a large number of Rákosi's former political prisoners, who had been reinstated as party functionaries and now seethed with enmity towards the Muscovite henchmen. Gerő tried to divert the wrath of the people by blaming past errors on Gábor Péter and his political police.

The riots in Poznan, Poland, in June of that year indicated that the time for a more forceful demonstration of national feelings had arrived. On 6 October, László Rajk and a few other victims of the show trials were reburied and rehabilitated. Thousands attended the ceremony, and it acted like a can of petrol on a smouldering fire.

On 23 October, students held a mass demonstration in Budapest. They demanded reforms, democratization and the return of Nagy. When they attempted to be heard over Hungarian radio, police tried to disperse them, using tear gas. They made several arrests. As the crowd struggled to free the students, police opened fire. Martial law was declared. Soviet troops were called in, and that same night their tanks were used against the demonstrators. The Revolution had begun.

For a short while it seemed that the people of Hungary might be victorious. But their Revolution and its dreams were to last for only twelve days before being crushed by the might of the Soviet Army. Thousands were killed, and thousands more, mainly students and young workers, were arrested or disappeared forever into the Soviet camps.

And so the deadly carousel went on . . .

*

Late in November 1956, Vali Rácz and Péter Halász left Hungary with their two small children. It was still possible to get out; the borders had not yet been entirely resealed. Like nearly a quarter of a million of their compatriots, they had had enough of oppression, censorship, lies and bloodshed.

172

Even so, it was a painful parting. Everything and everyone would have to be left behind. An unknown, new life would begin – the life of the refugee. Their ultimate goal was America: as ever, the symbol, the embodiment, of freedom.

They retrieved the cache of dollars from the old rabbit hutch at the end of the garden, where it had lain hidden between two wooden boards for a decade – Vali's earnings from the Café de la Paix. There were seventy dollars left. In the hyper-inflation of the post-war days, when it was illegal to possess dollars, that was a fabulous fortune.

But in the America of 1956, the 'treasure' from the rabbit hutch was a ludicrously paltry sum with which to start a new life. What the Yanks would no doubt have referred to as 'chicken feed'.

Sixteen

The morning of Sunday, 5 November 1989. Gölle, Transdanubia. The sun is so warm it could still be summer. In the middle of the village the old yellow-painted Catholic church with its curved spire stands out sharply against the bright blue sky. Its bells are ringing. It is a special day in Gölle.

This morning the new war memorial erected in the churchyard is to be officially unveiled, and Gölle's dead from the two world wars are to be honoured at a special mass. The parish priest, Ferenc Puska, has invited several outside guests to attend the mass, including some people not often seen in a church: such as the Rabbi of Pécs and the Secretary of the local branch of the Communist Party (previously known as the Hungarian Workers' Party, now magically transformed into the Western-style Hungarian Socialist Party).

The rabbi is there because the granite and marble memorial also records the names of the three Jews of Gölle, deported in the summer of 1944. At the start of the mass Father Puska welcomes the rabbi, and quotes the last known words of one of those Jews, 'Sad Gizella', the elderly spinster who'd clung to the railings at the end of her garden and cried, 'Don't take me! I'm Magyar, too!' Turning to the rabbi, who is sitting near the altar, he says, 'Yes, we are *all* Magyar, and they are all *our* dead.'

The mass begins. Hymns are sung. Up in the choir, the fine old organ once played by Ferenc Rácz is now played by the current cantor, old Kapinya, who, as a schoolboy before the war, was one of Rácz's pupils. His playing and singing cannot

174

match the artistry of his former headmaster, considered to have been the finest tenor in the Dunántúl. But if it weren't for Kapinya, there would be no cantor at all, because this position, once so highly regarded, has all but ceased to exist.

Later, Father Puska makes way for the older and more portly Auxiliary Bishop of Kaposvár, who is to deliver the sermon on this solemn occasion. He speaks at length, quotes from the Bible, employs parables, calls the congregation his 'brethren' and urges them to love one another. The village children in the front rows and the old women in the back listen attentively. The rabbi stifles a yawn, and his eyes wander up to the frescoes depicting the last supper, the crucifixion, the resurrection. He muses upon them with polite interest.

The bishop then administers Holy Communion. Many elderly widows, in black from their shoes to their head scarves, line up to receive the holy wafer. Afterwards, heads bent and hands clasped together, they shuffle back to their pews.

When the mass is over, the bishop and priest embrace the rabbi. It is a rare and touching moment. First the religious leaders, then the visiting dignitaries and guests, and finally the congregation silently file out and make their way around to the war memorial, at the side of the church. Many wreaths and vases of flowers have been placed at its base. It is time for the speeches of commemoration.

The bishop is first to speak. His gold robe gleams in the sunlight and billows gently with the breeze. Opposite him an altar boy holds aloft the Hungarian flag, recently relieved of the hammer and sickle. Next, the rabbi gives a moving and lyrical speech, expressing many humane sentiments. And he is followed by the head of the parish council, József Kovács. With his dark hair and doughy face, and standing before the granite monument in his sunglasses, Kovács bears a peculiar resemblance to Roy Orbison. He helped to bring about this day, by organizing the collection of the 150,000 forints (about £1,600) needed to build and erect the memorial. Ninety per cent of the money came from the villagers, the remaining ten per cent was donated by Vali Rácz.

Another speech is gravely read out by the representative of

175

the Somogy County branch of the People's Front, a political organization run under the auspices of the old Communist Party. The People's Front has no power any more. The 'People' have only scorn for this redundant tool of Communist oppression. But the old functionaries are loath to relinquish their semblance of authority.

When the ceremony is over, the bishop and the rabbi, together with their subordinates, retire across the road to the rectory, where Father Puska has laid on Sunday lunch. The crowd lingers awhile; neighbours and relatives greet each other. Rough-hewn country faces, old men with bowed legs and stubbly chins, gold-toothed grandmothers, sturdy younger women, simple and unadorned, and their unfussy, unfancy children who, impatient now, kick the gravel and shove each other, and laugh.

As they begin to disperse and go home to midday meals of their own, a middle-aged woman moves up to the memorial and puts a hand out to touch the black marble plaque engraved with the names of the dead. She searches for a particular name, and finding it, runs a finger across the letters. Suddenly she can contain her grief no longer. 'My dear, dead father!' she sobs loudly, not caring who hears her. 'How long ago it was that they took you from us!' Tears run down her face, but she does not wipe them away.

*

The wonderful thing about Gölle is that the twentieth century has done little to change it. Of course, modern technology has made its mandatory influence felt: in the sixties the peasants began to exchange their horse-drawn carts for automobiles and hot and cold running water became *de rigueur*; then, in the seventies, fridges and washing machines and televisions began to appear in the village. Now even videos are not uncommon. Over the past couple of decades, many of the nineteenth-century mudbrick houses have been pulled down and replaced; but the new houses don't look all that different.

Walking down the long central street of Gölle, flanked by rows of single-storey oblong houses, stuccoed and painted in

various fading pastel hues, the overall sensation is of timeless-
ness. Each house faces the road side-on, its narrow colonnaded
verandah overhung with vines. Behind it is the old brick barn:
traditionally the farmer's animals, vital to his livelihood, were
housed first and with the best materials; his family's mudbrick
home came afterwards. Beyond the barn, stretching out into
the distance, are the fertile fields. A black cloud of crows
suddenly appears overhead – they've been nicknamed 'Rumanian pheasants', because the appalling food shortages in that
country have turned even the lowly crow into fair game for the
dinner table.

In the space between the houses are those fabulous Trans-
danubian farmyards which are a riot of ducks and dogs,
chickens and kittens and geese, all coexisting happily amongst
the multi-coloured flowering shrubs, ancient wells, wine cellars, wood piles, pigsties and smoke-houses, beneath owl-laden
trees and hanging strings of hot red *paprikas* drying in the sun. It
has always been so.

Old women in aprons and headscarves potter about in them,
too, their hands like thick, gnarled roots. They spend their
entire lives at work – with the soil, with the animals, in the
kitchen, and tending to the grandchildren. And when they are
not working, these self-appointed guardians of the dead slowly
wend their way to the village cemetery, to pray at the graves of
their loved ones. There are no old people's homes in Gölle. No
meals-on-wheels or bingo. Here they simply carry on, business
as usual, until they die, the men and women both. And they all
look ten or fifteen years older than their age.

The first of November was All Saints' Day, followed by the
'Day of the Dead' on the second. The cemetery is ablaze with
the floral offerings which, by tradition, are on that day placed
on the graves of family members. There are chrysanthemums
of every colour, bright carnations and pansies. There is a stone
monument in the cemetery, a memorial to the victims of
Central Europe's last great cholera epidemic in the early
nineteenth century. It bears a statue of Jesus on the cross, above
a skull and crossbones. Underneath it is the local victims' mass
grave. Behind the monument, on top of a little mound, is the

old yellow chapel used on holy days and special occasions. Its fresco was painted in 1928 by the ecclesiastical artist Sándor Éber, a distant relative of Vali's. It had badly deteriorated over the years and not long ago Vali commissioned the German artist Gisela Oberbeck to restore it. Now it is clean and vivid once more.

Vali's childhood home, the headmaster's house (the oldest in the village), is also in need of attention. It is to house the 'Vali Rácz Museum', due to open in the spring, but the rooms have to be renovated first. The thick, 300-year-old stone walls are damp, and Vali Rácz refuses to put her cherished memorabilia in them until they are dry. Kovács, of the parish council, is responsible for organizing the repairs and supervising the preparations, and he has assured her that everything will go smoothly. The plastering and painting will be done, the new heating system will be in place, the specially built display cases will be ready, the marble plaque will be up . . .

But he has other things on his mind, too. Local council elections are coming up early next year. For the first time in four decades, a Communist victory is not a foregone conclusion. People of all political persuasions may now run for office, and Kovács knows that, even though he is no longer a Communist, he is tainted by his past and his chances of success are slim. The peasantry of Gölle has deserted the Communist Party *en masse* – there were 125 members in the village, now there are five.

So Kovács has been making contingency plans. If he loses his job on the council, he is going to become a snail-breeder. It seems a bizarre enterprise, but he explains that it is a highly lucrative business, which requires little in the way of capital investment. Apparently, Hungary is a great place to breed snails. He has already sent away for some kind of instruction book, and made contact with an exporting firm. Needless to say, his snails would be bred purely for export to other European countries. A Hungarian wouldn't think of eating a snail.

The local collective, like the Communist Party, has begun its disintegration. In 1948 it swallowed up endless hectares of smallholders' farmland, allowing each family to keep only a small tract of land for its own use. It has always been an inefficient institution in which hard-working, productive farmers are penalized by having to subsidize the ineffective ones, and are thus discouraged from being productive. Now these state collectives are only too eager to return the land to private ownership. Each family will soon be able to claim back the same amount of land as was taken from it forty-one years ago.

The problem is that not many of them want it. How can they transform themselves overnight into capitalist farmers once more, without any capital? Few of them could afford the sophisticated, expensive equipment needed for a large farm, or to take on paid labourers. The older generation, who knew how to work the land and make it flourish, are too old now to start again. The younger generations have trained for other things; many of them have left the countryside altogether in favour of towns and cities. They aren't interested in the responsibility of land ownership. A new smallholders' stratum must emerge from somewhere else – perhaps from amongst the burgeoning class of urban entrepreneurs, many of whom are becoming disillusioned with city life.

But all of these radical, previously unthinkable political changes are as nothing compared to the *real* news in Gölle: at long last, in 1989, the village has been brought into the national telephone network. Until this year the only phone was at the council offices, just like during the war, when Ferenc Rácz had to go there to make that urgent call to his daughter in Budapest because of the dangerous rumours about Ilona. Now about a third of the 450 homes in Gölle have new lines far superior to those in many parts of the capital. And old widow Rozsi, whose son emigrated many years ago to Florida, can just lift up the receiver and call his home in Sarasota any time she likes. For her, that is the greatest miracle of the year.

Beyond the little world of Gölle, with its church bells and drying *paprikas*, where in so many ways life goes on as it did a hundred years ago under the Habsburgs, there are extraordinary things afoot. The Hungarian nation is being rocked by another Revolution – a peaceful one, this time. Each day brings a new announcement – Hungary wants to be neutral, to leave the Warsaw Pact, Hungary is applying for membership of the Common Market, Hungary would like to join the European Parliament. Otto Habsburg is interested in running for President of the new Hungarian Republic in the national elections of 1990. Russian is no longer compulsory in schools. The red star has disappeared from the top of the Parliament building – it took two days to saw it off and lift it away by helicopter to oblivion . . .

The new constitution, written and approved by an eighty-eight-per-cent majority in Parliament, contains the following passage: 'No social organization, state organ or citizen can endeavour to seize or exercise power by force, or to possess power exclusively. Every person is legally entitled, and indeed obliged, to resist such endeavours . . .'

But the economy is a wreck. Inflation is soaring and times are very hard. Old-age pensioners, their paltry, stagnating pensions useless against the annual twenty-per-cent rate of inflation, are skirting around the edge of starvation. The Hungarians are worn out and frustrated by the endless talk and chaos generated by the new freedom. New political parties are cropping up the whole time, but there is great apprehension – who knows what will happen? Which party and which leader will emerge to drag the country out of its terrible predicament? What do these newcomers to democracy know about managing a nation and its economy? And meanwhile, the standard of living steadily deteriorates. These are the dire labour pains of democracy.

The last time a Hungarian democracy was born, at the end of the war, it, too, emerged out of a disaster – the disaster of a tragic national defeat. That first democracy was killed in its infancy. Now it is emerging out of the disaster of four decades of repression in the Soviet bloc. Perhaps this second attempt will succeed. It would be about time, too. Hungary has always believed itself to be manifestly a part of the West, ever since the tenth century when Prince Géza, Chieftain of the Magyar tribe, turned his back on the Byzantine Empire of the East and bound his nation's destiny to the world of Rome.

That was a millennium ago. Will the emerging new political

order in Europe allow Hungary's destiny to be fulfilled? The Hungarians, after all, have played no small part in the creation of this new order. Theirs was the first Soviet bloc country to tinker with *glasnost* and *perestroika* (even before Gorbachev had sanctioned them). Their bold, unprecedented act of throwing open the border to the flood of East Germans seeking freedom was the catalyst which brought the Berlin Wall crashing down, literally overnight, bringing the Politburo with it, which in turn led to the mass demonstrations and dramatic changes in neighbouring Czechoslovakia. Now there are tremors in Bulgaria . . . Where will it all end? As yet, that is unclear. But, without doubt, this is one 'domino theory' which will not remain merely a theory.

*

Early one Sunday morning, shortly before Christmas 1988, Vali Rácz had a sublime experience. It happened in the Gellért Hotel, where she was staying during a visit to Budapest.

Her new *glasnost*-fame was just beginning to blossom, and more and more people were approaching her for interviews. Her name was once again in circulation after the long decades of obscurity and neglect.

For the first time since the early fifties she had been inside a Hungarian radio studio. The producer of a popular weekly magazine programme had invited her on to his show, to talk about herself and reminisce about her career. They had taped the interview a few days earlier and Vali was told that their colourful, informal discussion, inter-spliced with some of her old records, was scheduled for broadcast on that Sunday's programme.

Vali had her alarm clock set for six a.m., when the two-hour programme came on the air. Now, when it woke her up, she made a great effort to get out of bed. She was tired from the previous evening's lively and protracted supper with friends, from all the talking and joking and the blare of the gypsy orchestra. And, as usual, she had her aches and pains. Normally she would have slept late – her one habitual concession to her years. But she didn't want to miss the show. She switched on the radio.

She put on her dressing gown and slippers, dashed a little water over her face, then went over to the tall window to pull aside the curtains. She was staying in her customary room, a spacious third-floor bedroom with a tiny balcony overlooking the busy square before the hotel, with the fine view of the river and Pest beyond it. Dawn had not yet broken, but its promise hung in the air; the city was still sprinkled with night-time lights, the moon still shone and lay reflected in the waters of the Danube. She yawned, groggy from sleep.

She was standing by the window, leaning on her cane and gazing out at the view, when she heard her name announced on the radio. The interview began. It flowed well – she spoke in an easy, relaxed manner, answering the questions put to her with wit and charm. It was strange, being on Hungarian radio again.

Then they played the first of her old records. A little scratched and crackly, her voice was warm and resonant, nevertheless. It was one of those popular, romantic *chansons* from the early years of the war, which were linked to her name and epitomized that era of long ago. The voice from the past, with its many associations, filled Room 312 of the Hotel Gellért.

And that was when it happened. After so many years, listening once more to herself singing on the radio had a most unexpected effect. All at once, through some overpowering mystical force, the past and the present came together and fused. Just as the city which lay before her was caught in the brief and ethereal balance between night and day, for a few minutes, while the song was on, Vali Rácz existed in an intoxicating state without time, without age.

Not quite sure whether she was still in this world or had already entered the next, she felt herself departing from her physical being altogether – the white hair and cane disappeared. She was both old and wise, and young and beautiful. She was fulfilled.

Postscript

Of the Jews who hid in Vali's house during the Nazi Occupation, only two are alive today: Margit Herzog and Ilona (this is not her real name; she prefers anonymity). They both remarried after the war and, by coincidence, settled in West Germany, where their husbands decided to work. They are now widowed and live not far from each other. Margit has survived her daughter Marietta, who died from cancer tragically young a few years ago.

The Mandels emigrated in 1946, first to Australia but eventually ending up in Tel Aviv, where they continued to run their business. They had a brief reunion with Vali in London in 1972 and corresponded with her to the end of their lives a few years later.

Vera Somló, after a distinguished career in publishing, has recently started to write her wartime memoirs. This has unfortunately been interrupted by a serious illness. She still lives in the same flat which she occupied during the war, surrounded by the same antique furniture, bulging bookshelves and walls covered with her collection of old Hungarian paintings. She still enjoys reading the French classics. Recently, she and Vali saw each other for the first time since their dramatic meeting at the Café de la Paix in 1945.

Mihály Szüle emigrated to America in 1946, when his theatre was closed down, but four decades later he moved back to Budapest with his second wife. With their US pensions, puny by American standards, they are able to live lavishly in

Hungary. He is now, at eighty-seven, the last living Hungarian theatre director from before the war.

József, Vali's doctor and admirer, who had been so kind and helpful during those difficult months in 1944, died not long after the war from a terminal illness. It was a tragic irony that, having survived such perils under the Nazis, he was to die so soon after being liberated.

Károly, Paul Barabás's son, kept in touch with Vali for several years after the war. She naturally took an interest in Paul's only child and helped him in any way she could. Then, in 1950 at the age of nineteen, he emigrated to Paris, where he joined the US Army, eventually became an American citizen, and began a career in UNICEF. Just before he left, he went to say goodbye to Vali and her husband, Péter. The thin, pale young man had very little money. Péter gave him some cash and an overcoat. For a while he wrote to them from Paris. Then his letters stopped.

Ferenc Fiala, the Arrow Cross press chief who played a part in Vali's release from the Majestic, died only last year at the age of eighty-four. After the war he was sentenced to death, but through the intervention of the writer Paul Ignótus, his sentence was commuted to a long term of imprisonment. He was released in 1956 and emigrated to West Germany. There he wrote several books about wartime Hungary, and remained unrepentant to the last.

Of the fate of Sasha, Vali knows nothing. Over the years, she would occasionally remember their time together and wonder what became of him and whether he was still alive. He would be in his eighties today, a grandparent like Vali. And his life would have spanned a phenomenal century in Russian history: from the Bolshevik Revolution to Gorbachev.

Vali and Péter Halász lived in America until 1970. Vali gave occasional concerts in various Western cities for large gatherings of Hungarian *émigrés*, who remembered well the *chanteuse* from the old days. But her career was essentially over. Her main role was that of mother and housewife. No one knew, in the supermarkets of suburban New York, that the middle-aged woman pushing a trolley was once a glamorous film star. It was to be a long, arduous exile, but she was not embittered by it. She took great pleasure in gardening, just as she had in Budapest, and in running her modern, all–American kitchen. (It was only after the age of forty-five that she began to cook; she eventually excelled in the art.)

Then at last they moved back to Europe. Now they are domiciled in West Germany, where, until his recent retirement, Péter was the mainstay of Radio Free Europe's Hungarian Section. His work for the radio, over a period of thirty years, won him generations of listeners in every stratum of society in Hungary, and among the vast Hungarian *émigré* population throughout the free world. He has also had many books published in the West since 1956. This year, by virtue of the new era of *glasnost*, he has been approached by more than one of the new independent publishing houses in Budapest, keen to bring out his earlier works. He has nothing against this, but neither does he view his 'rehabilitation' with anything more than cynical detachment. He has vowed never to return to the country of his birth. For him, and countless others of his generation, the new democratic Hungary has come rather late in the day.

Vali's house on Budakeszi Avenue played a central role in this story of what happened in Budapest that year of 1944–5. It bore witness to a series of events and changes which would have been unthinkable before the war. Vali managed to hold on to it even after the Communist nationalizations, by keeping it fully occupied. As it was in her parents' name, the state could not take it away when she and Péter escaped after the Revolution.

Vali finally sold the house a few years ago to the parents of wealthy tennis champion Andrea Temesvári. They had it modernized and altered beyond recognition. Then they sold it at a hefty profit to the government of Colombia, to be used as that country's embassy. Now the Colombian flag billows in the breeze in front of the house at 47d. Somehow that seems most bizarre.

185

Chronology

1944

19 March:	German troops occupy Hungary
21 March:	Eichmann arrives in Budapest
22 March:	Horthy forced to appoint Sztójay to head the Hungarian government
3 April:	Yellow Star Decree issued
14 May:	Commencement of deportations in the countryside
17 May:	Joel Brand leaves for Istanbul on the 'trucks for lives' mission
30 June:	1,700 Jews allowed to leave for Switzerland
8 July:	Last day of deportations
9 July:	Wallenberg arrives in Budapest
14 July:	Eichmann and Baky attempt to deport 1,500 inmates of Kistarcsa
23 August:	Following a *coup d'état* in Rumania, Horthy resolves to dismiss Sztójay and appoint General Lakatos in his place
24 August:	Eichmann and his *Sonderkommando* leave Budapest
8 September:	A government decree bans music in public places
15 October:	Horthy's announcement of Hungary's withdrawal from the Axis camp is followed by Szálasi's *coup d'état*

17 October:	Eichmann returns to Budapest
8 November:	Beginning of death marches to Hegyeshalom
23 November:	Hitler orders the German High Command in Budapest not to surrender the city at any cost
25 November:	Arrow Cross government invokes martial law against the families of army deserters
8 December:	The flight of the Arrow Cross government to Sopron is now complete
10 December:	The Budapest ghetto, containing approximately 70,000 Jews, is closed. Szálasi orders the immediate conscription of all males aged between fourteen and seventy
21 December:	First session of the Provisional National Assembly in Debrecen
23 December:	Eichmann flees Budapest. Provisional Government declares war on Germany
24 December:	Soviet Army surrounds Budapest
27 December:	All Budapest theatres and cinemas close down. A curfew forbids citizens to be out between five p.m. and seven a.m.
29 December:	Soviet High Command issues ultimatum to German and Hungarian forces. Two Soviet envoys are accidentally killed

1945

13 January:	Red Army enters Pest
17 January:	The ghetto is liberated. The Germans retreat to Buda, blowing up the bridges behind them. Wallenberg is abducted by Soviet authorities
20 January:	Hungary concludes armistice treaty with the Allies in Moscow
11 February:	At eight p.m. a breakout is attempted by the defenders of the Castle
13 February:	Remainder of German-Hungarian resistance in Buda is crushed

25 February:	Rákosi addresses the workers of the capital
15 March:	Land Reform Bill is issued
29 March:	Anti-Jewish discrimination is outlawed
4 April:	The war is over in Hungary
13 April:	The Provisional Government moves to the capital
24 June:	Hungary's war reparations to Russia are set at $200,000,000, to be repaid by January 1951
30 September:	USA and USSR recognize the Hungarian government
3 October:	Eleven major Hungarian war criminals are flown home by the US military authorities
7 October:	Smallholders' Party wins majority in Budapest municipal elections
4 November:	Smallholders' Party wins majority in general election
17 November:	Great Britain recognizes the Hungarian government

Bibliography

BARTLETT, Vernon, *East of the Iron Curtain*, Latimer House, London, 1949

BISS, Andre, *A Million Jews to Save*, Hutchinson, London, 1973

BRAHAM, Randolph L., *The Destruction of Hungarian Jewry*, World Federation of Hungarian Jews, New York, 1963

BRAHAM, Randolph L. and VÁGÓ, Béla (eds.), *The Holocaust in Hungary: Forty Years Later*, Columbia University Press, New York, 1985

GLATZ, Ferenc (ed.), *Az 1944 Év Históriája*, A Lapkiadó Vállalat, Budapest, 1984

GOSZTONYI, Péter, *Magyarország a második világháboruban III*, Herp Verlag, Munich, 1987

GUNTHER, John, *Behind the Curtain*, Harper & Brothers, New York, 1948

HANDLER, Andrew (ed. and trans.), *The Holocaust in Hungary: An Anthology of Jewish Response*, University of Alabama Press, Alabama, 1982

KATZBURG, Nathaniel, *Hungary and the Jews: Policy and Legislation 1920–1943*, Bar-Ilan University Press, Israel, 1981

KOVÁCS, Imre (ed.), *Facts about Hungary: The Fight for Freedom*, The Hungarian Committee, New York, 1966

LÉVAI, Jenő, *Black Book on the Martyrdom of Hungarian Jewry*, The Central European Times Publishing Co., Zurich, 1948

LÉVAI, Jenő (ed.), *Eichmann in Hungary*, Pannonia Press, Budapest, 1961

LÉVAI, Jenő, *Fehér Könyv: Külföldi Akciók Magyar Zsidók Mentésére*, Officina, Budapest, 1946

LUKÁCS, John, *Budapest 1900: A Historical Portrait of a City and its Culture*, Weidenfeld & Nicolson, New York, 1988

MASTERS, Anthony, *The Summer that Bled: The Biography of Hannah Senesh*, Michael Joseph, London, 1972

PHILLIPS, John, *Bled to the Gutter: A Photo-reporter's Story*, Weidenfeld & Nicolson, London, 1959

SANDBERG, Moshe, *My Longest Year: In the Hungarian Labour Service and in the Nazi Camps*, Yad Vashem, Jerusalem, 1968

SHIRER, William L., *The Nightmare Years*, Little, Brown & Co., Boston, 1984

SZÁSZ, Béla, *Volunteers for the Gallows: Anatomy of a Show Trial*, Chatto & Windus, London, 1971

WEISSBERG, Alex, *Advocate for the Dead: The Story of Joel Brand*, André Deutsch, London, 1958

ZINNER, Tibor and RÓNA, Péter, *Szálasiék bilincsben*, A Lapkiadó Vállalat, Budapest, 1986

Index

Gergely, Sándor, 15–16, 150

Germany: invasion of Hungary, 4–5, 17–18; dominates Hungary, 37; 'Operation Panzerfaust', 53; 'Magyar Evening' concert in Berlin, 56–8; Hungary declares war on, 87; Siege of Budapest, 88, 93–108, 110

Gerő, Ernő, 99–100, 128, 171–2

Gestapo, 4–5, 22, 65–9, 76, 80, 144, 154

Géza, Prince, 180

Gille, General, 97

Gölle, 6–7, 8–11, 32, 40–3, 46–7, 52, 85, 94–5, 114, 134–5, 162, 174–9

Gömbös, Gyula, 34–5

Gorbachev, Mikhail, 181

Grassy, József, 159

Győr, 7

Habsburg, Otto, 180

Hain, Péter, 26, 64, 70, 72–3, 76–80, 83, 115, 116–17, 127, 137, 157–8

Halász, Péter, 162, 172–3, 184–5

Hangli Kioszk, Budapest, 13–16, 17–18, 32, 56, 150

Harsányi, Zsolt, 15

Harway, Lilian, 57

Háy, Gyula, 161

Hegyeshalom, 59, 61, 108, 117

Herzog, Feri, 29, 145

Herzog, Gyuri, 145

Herzog, Ignác, 27

Herzog, Imre, 29, 54, 141–2, 145

Herzog, Margit, 27–30, 33, 51, 60, 65–6, 67–8, 70, 73, 140–1, 142–6, 183

Herzog, Sándor, 27, 28–9, 145, 150

Himmler, Heinrich, 25, 26, 40, 44, 82

Hitler, Adolf, 17, 25, 34, 35, 36–7, 39, 44, 59, 62, 88, 96, 105–6, 130, 161

Horthy, István, 32

Horthy, Admiral Nicholas, 5, 17, 35–7, 39, 40, 44–5, 52–3, 160

Hotel Adlon, Berlin, 57

Hotel Majestic, Budapest, 26, 64, 69, 70–6, 80, 116–17, 137, 153–4, 167–8

Hull, Cordell, 37–8

Hullamosó pub, Budapest, 21

Hugária Gumi Textil, 24

Hungarian Army, 33–4, 62, 148, 159

Hungarian People's Court, 99, 157, 160, 163

Hungarian Radio, 52, 172, 181–2

Hungarian Secret Police, 26

Hungarian Socialist Party, 174

Hungarian Workers' Party, 165, 174

Hungarista Party, 139

Ignótus, Paul, 184

Illustrated Army Camp News, 33

Ilona, 40–1, 42, 46–8, 51, 53, 60, 67, 135, 140, 146–8, 183

Imrédy, Béla, 36–7, 157, 158

Independence Party, 164–5

International War Crimes Tribunal, 158

Irodalmi Újság, 171

Istanbul, 39

Italy, 13, 37

János (gardener), 83–5, 118

Jány, Gusztáv, 159

Japan, 37

Japán Coffee House, Budapest, 161–2
Jaross, Andor, 157
Jesuits, 95–6, 120–1
Jewish Council, 40
Jewish Rescue Committee, 39, 144
Jews: Nazi invasion of Hungary, 4–5; Third Jewish Law, 16; Kállay government protects, 17; Vali hides, 20–5, 30, 40, 51–2, 63–4; deportation from Hungary, 25–6, 38; anti-Semitism in Hungary, 34–7; Horthy stops deportations, 39–40, 44–5; deportations from Hungary resumed, 54–5, 59–61; Wallenberg's work to save, 60–2; massacres in Budapest, 81–3; Budapest ghetto survives, 82–3, 98–9; accuse Vali of collaborating with Nazis, 116–23
József (doctor) 48–9, 60–1, 65–6, 69, 71, 76, 79, 134, 184
József, Attila, 12
Juan les Pins, 13
Jüttner, General Hans, 59

Kádár, János, 166–7
Kállay, Miklós, 17, 55, 149
Kapinya, 174–5
Kaposvár, 9, 10, 70
Kaposvár, Auxiliary Bishop of, 175–6
Kasztner, Rezső, 39
Keleti, Dezső, 30, 140–1, 144
Keleti, Péter, 28, 30, 73, 140, 144–5
Kemény, Egon, 12
Kemény, Gábor, 61

Kerekes, János, 12
Khrushchev, Nikita, 169–70
Kistarcsa camp, 40
Kodály, Zoltán, 12
Kóhner, Baroness, 111–12, 119, 124–5, 151
Kolozsvár, 19
Kornfeld family, 27
Kossuth Bridge, 161
Kovács, Béla, 163
Kovács, József, 175, 178
Kovács, Mr, 83, 91, 118
Kroll State Opera House, Berlin, 56
Kun, Father András, 80, 137–8, 139, 158–9, 168
Kun, Béla, 34, 35, 36, 129–30

Labour Party (Britain), 130
Lakatos, General Géza, 44, 52
Land Reform Bill, 130
Lázár, Mária, 87
League of Nations, 35
Lehár, Franz, 15
Lenin, 129
Life Magazine, 133
Lloyd George, David, 9
Losonc, 27, 28
Luftwaffe, 98

'Magyar Evening', Berlin (1943), 56, 57, 77
Magyar Stage Play, 48
Malinovsky, General, 105, 110
Mandel, Jenő, 21, 22–5, 40, 51–2, 60, 67, 140, 146–7, 169, 183
Mandel, Szerén, 24–5, 40, 51–2, 60, 67, 140, 146–7, 167, 169, 183
Manfred Weiss Works, 27
Márai, Sándor, 131–2

of Budapest, 88–9, 90–108, 109–11; under Khrushchev, 169–70; crushes Hungarian Revolution, 172

Special Operations Commando, 25–6, 45

Spider's Web, 11

SS, 26–7, 55, 57, 59, 81, 94, 146, 149

Stalin, Joseph, 1, 99, 110, 129–30, 152, 161, 165–7, 168, 169

Steinmetz, 93–4

Strasshof, 54

Sweden, 60

Swedish Legation, 49, 60–1

Szabad Nép, 165

Szakasits, Árpád, 165

Szálasi, Ferenc, 52–3, 64, 77, 81, 106, 142, 157, 160

Széchenyi family, 27

Székesfehérvár, 86

Szenkár, Dezső, 12

Szenkár, Jenő, 12

Szép, Ernő, 12

Szívós, 99

Szombathelyi, Ferenc, 159

Sztójay, Döme, 17, 44, 56, 57, 77, 157, 158

Szüle, Mihály, 45–6, 70, 72, 87, 98, 183–4

Teleki, Count Géza, 128

Teleki, Count Paul, 37, 128–9

Temesvári, Andrea, 185

Terézkörúti Theatre, 12, 13

Third Jewish Law, 16

Tildy, Zoltán, 156, 165

Tito, Marshal, 165

Tolbuchin, General, 97

Tolna, 7

Tolnay, Klári, 21, 111

Trade Union Council, 156

Transdanubia, 97, 114

Transylvania, 19

Trianon, Treaty of, 35

Tripartite Pact, 37

Turks, 87

UFA Studios, 21, 57

Ujvidék, 159

Ukrainian Fronts, 97–8, 105

United States of America, 37–8, 39, 76, 97, 130–1, 132, 160, 173, 184–5

US Army, 156

Vajna, Gábor, 54, 65, 158

Vali Rácz Museum, 2, 178

Van Dyck, 26

Varga, Monseigneur Béla, 163

Vas, Zoltán, 99–100

Veesenmayer, Edmund, 4, 26, 44, 158

Venice, 13

Vidám Theatre, Budapest, 45, 48, 55, 70, 72, 83

Vienna, 6, 15, 54, 62, 106

Vigadó Concert Hall, Budapest, 4, 17, 32

Villon, François, 12–13, 14, 149

Vörös, General, 62

Voroshilov, Marshal Kliment, 131, 156, 164

Wachsman, Dr, 41

Wachsman sisters, 41–2

Waffen-SS, 84, 97–8

Waldsee, 29, 145

Wallenberg, Raoul, 49, 60–2, 69, 75, 76, 82–3, 97, 139

Warsaw, 109–110

Warsaw Pact, 180

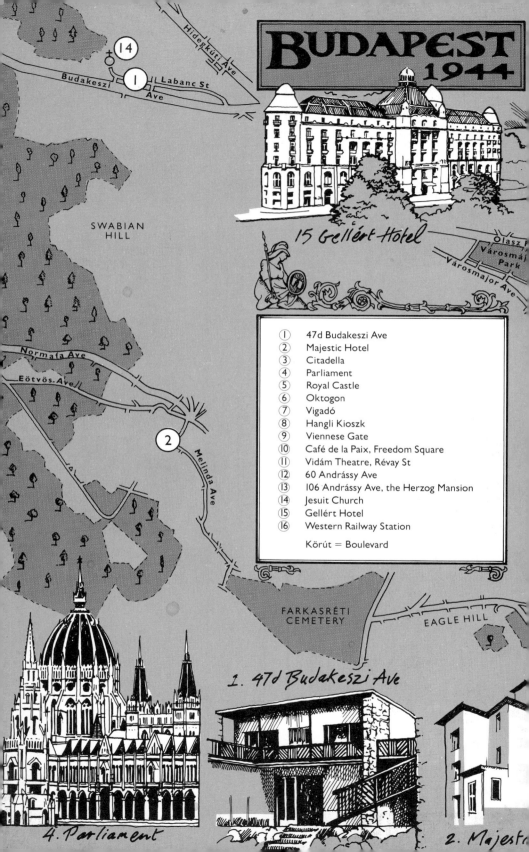